INTELLIGENT POLICING

DEDICATION

I would like to dedicate the book to my three beautiful grandchildren Gabrielle, Gracie and Theo

To order our books please go to our website www.criticalpublishing.com or contact our distributor Ingram Publisher Services, telephone 01752 202301 or email IPSUK.orders@ingramcontent.com. Details of bulk order discounts can be found at www. criticalpublishing.com/delivery-information.

Our titles are also available in electronic format: for individual use via our website and for libraries and other institutions from all the major ebook platforms.

INTELLIGENCE-LED POLICING

THE PROFESSIONAL POLICING CURRICULUM IN PRACTICE

CRAIG HUGHES

SERIES EDITOR: TONY BLOCKLEY

CRITICAL
PUBLISHING

First published in 2023 by Critical Publishing Ltd

British Library Cataloguing in Publication Data
A CIP record for this book is available from the British Library

ISBN: 978-1-915080-20-2

This book is also available in the following e-book formats:
EPUB ISBN: 978-1-915080-21-9
Adobe e-book ISBN: 978-1-915080-22-6

Cover and text design by Out of House Limited
Project management by Newgen Publishing UK
Printed and bound in Great Britain by 4edge, Essex

Critical Publishing
3 Connaught Road
St Albans
AL3 5RX

Printed on FSC
accredited paper

CONTENTS

ABOUT THE SERIES EDITOR

TONY BLOCKLEY

Tony Blockley is the lead for policing at Leeds Trinity University, responsible for co-ordinating policing higher education, including developing programmes and enhancing the current provision in line with the Policing Education Qualifications Framework (PEQF) and supporting the College of Policing. He served within policing for over 30 years, including a role as Chief Superintendent and Head of Crime.

ABOUT THE AUTHOR

CRAIG HUGHES

Craig Hughes is Head of Policing at the University of Derby. He specialises in teaching financial and digital intelligence and investigation using evidence-based principles, drawing on 31 years of policing experience.

FOREWORD

Police professionalism has seen significant developments over recent years, including the implementation of the Vision 2025 and the establishment of the Policing Education Qualifications Framework (PEQF). There is no doubt that policing has become complex, and this complexity and its associated challenges are increasing day by day with greater scrutiny, expectations and accountability. The educational component of police training and development therefore allows officers to gain a greater understanding and appreciation of the theories and activities associated with high-quality policing provision.

The scholastic element of the Vision 2025 provides an opportunity to engage in meaningful insight and debate around some of the most sensitive areas of policing while also applying lessons from the past to develop the service for the future. While there are many books and articles on numerous subjects associated with policing, this new series – *The Professional Policing Curriculum in Practice* – provides an insightful opportunity to start that journey. It distils the key concepts and topics within policing into an accessible format, combining theory and practice to provide you with a secure basis of knowledge and understanding.

Policing is now a degree-level entry profession, which has provided a unique opportunity to develop fully up-to-date books for student and trainee police officers that focus on the content of the PEQF curriculum, are tailored specifically to the new pre-join routes, and reflect the diversity and complexity of twenty-first-century society. Each book is stand-alone, but the books also work together to layer information as you progress through your programme. The pedagogical features of the books have been carefully designed to improve your understanding and critical thinking skills within the context of policing. They include learning objectives, case studies, evidence-based practice examples, critical thinking and reflective activities, and summaries of key concepts. Each chapter also includes a guide to further reading, meaning you don't have to spend hours of research to find that piece of information you are looking for.

Information and intelligence are often used interchangeably within policing but are significantly different. This book examines the distinction between the two and, importantly, provides an understanding of their intentions and purpose for effective policing. Through a wider lens, the book explores the relationship between information, intelligence and investigation, creating investigative opportunities that are available for all police officers and staff irrespective of rank or role.

The book develops a knowledge base, exploring the concept of intelligence as it applies to strategic, tactical and practical levels of operational policing (integrating with evidence-based policing). It considers the parallels in terms of provenance and checking intelligence in an operational setting and how those processes and understandings correlate with academic research.

Having been involved in policing for over 40 years, the benefits of these books are obvious to me: I see them becoming the go-to guides for the PEQF curriculum across all the various programmes associated with the framework, while also having relevance for more experienced officers.

Tony Blockley
Discipline Head: Policing
Leeds Trinity University

CHAPTER 1
INFORMATION AND INTELLIGENCE

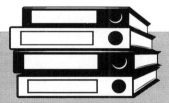

LEARNING OBJECTIVES

AFTER READING THIS CHAPTER YOU WILL BE ABLE TO:

- ⚙ understand the concepts of information, intelligence and intelligence-led policing;

- ⚙ identify the key parts of the intelligence cycle;

- ⚙ explain why sources of information need to be checked and sourced;

- ⚙ define the terms 'strategic' and 'operational' intelligence;

- ⚙ explain the similarities between intelligence gathering and a research project;

- ⚙ understand the need to establish the provenance of all information sources used to produce intelligence.

INTRODUCTION

A quick search on the internet will reveal that intelligence is a much-discussed topic which, so far, has not resulted in a universally accepted definition of what it actually is. This chapter introduces and considers the concepts of information, intelligence and intelligence-led policing to enable you to begin to develop an understanding of the basic considerations when engaged in intelligence practice.

Throughout the chapter, we examine the general concepts of intelligence and how it is divided into strategic intelligence and operational intelligence. We then consider how intervention points (where action can be taken) are the desired outcome from intelligence assessment. Routine collection of information is examined against the structure of an information analysis framework (the intelligence cycle) before considering the dangers of too much information, the definition and deployment of Covert Human Intelligence Sources (CHIS), surveillance opportunities to gather intelligence, and the emergence of the internet as a current risk and threat environment. Examples throughout the chapter underpin the general importance of understanding the difference between information and intelligence as well as highlighting the impact of intelligence usage to develop robust and lawful policing practice. Finally, parallels between intelligence gathering and research projects are identified and explained – checking the source, defining the origin and testing the rigor of information, so it can be relied upon and used effectively.

CRITICAL THINKING ACTIVITY 1.1

LEVEL 4

Imagine you are on duty on a rural beat when a member of the public who is out walking the dog approaches you. During the ensuing conversation you are told that the barn in a nearby collection of farm buildings is being used to store plant machinery stolen from building sites. The farmer's name is Jackson and the dog walker thinks he has been 'done before' for handling stolen goods. The dog walker refuses to provide any personal details and does not want to get involved but thought you ought to know.

Is what you have been told information or intelligence? Whether you understand the difference or not, the real question is: What are you going to do with what you have been told?

*   Decide whether what you have been told is information or intelligence and the next steps you would take.

Sample answers are provided at the end of this book.

INFORMATION SOURCES

The dictionary definition of information usually defines it as something which originates from investigation, study or instruction (Merriam-Webster, 2022). Virtually anything can be construed as information but in policing terms it is possible to group information sources into three broad headings:

1. information which already exists (including all written and electronic sources);

2. information generated by law enforcement – such as general observations, patrol duties, surveillance or CHIS (informants);

3. information from witnesses or victims – resulting from a crime or other event – or from a member of the public.

Within each of these three areas, the possibilities for information retrieval are endless. The key is what happens to the information once you have identified and obtained it and how it might become intelligence. Wherever your information is sourced from, always check and corroborate it as a rule of thumb. For example, you never want to be in a position where you execute a search warrant at the wrong address because the intelligence was faulty.

WHAT IS INTELLIGENCE?

This seems to be a simple question but the answer is not as straightforward as you might think. The reason is that in both academic and law enforcement terms, there remains no universally accepted definition. Academics have debated its definition for many years and each law enforcement agency worldwide seems to have its own understanding of how the concept of intelligence can be explained and what is meant if the term is used. The real problem seems to be that the terms 'information' and 'intelligence' are often used interchangeably. Collecting information is often incorrectly referred to as collecting intelligence (Petersen, 2005). This wrongly implies they are the same thing. '*It is what people do with data and information that gives them the special quality that we casually call intelligence*' (Warner, 2002, p 15). In other words, information is collected but analysis of that information produces intelligence.

To give you an idea of the way in which the definitions of intelligence can vary, Table 1.1 contains a few examples.

Table 1.1 Different definitions of 'intelligence'

Agency	Intelligence definition
Federal Bureau of Investigation (USA)	Defines intelligence as refined information which is useful to policy makers concerned with threats to national security (FBI, 2022).
National Crime Agency (UK)	More widely defines intelligence as '*information which has been analysed to assess its relevance and reliability*' (National Crime Agency, 2022a).
The United Nations Office on Drugs and Crime	Defines intelligence in a similar vein but also includes any added value and the context of its source and reliability (UNODC, 2011).
The former Association of Chief Police Officers (ACPO), now the National Police Chiefs' Council (NPCC)	Provides perhaps the best working definition: '*information that has been subject to a defined evaluation and risk assessment process in order to assist with police decision making*' (ACPO, 2005, p 13).

For the purposes of this chapter, it is the ACPO (now NPCC) definition which is referred to.

REFLECTIVE PRACTICE 1.1

LEVEL 4

- Think of three national or international law enforcement agencies and then browse their websites. Find their definitions of intelligence and consider whether their interpretation has been influenced by their mandate (what they were created to do).

- Search for any academic article or book about intelligence and compare the law enforcement agency definitions you have chosen with how academic commentators describe intelligence. Notice that intelligence, in the absence of any legal definition, is more often than not a matter of context (how it applies to the role being undertaken).

Sample answers are provided at the end of this book

OPERATIONAL AND STRATEGIC INTELLIGENCE

From a practical aspect, intelligence is usually divided into two main categories, operational (tactical) and strategic (Richards, 2010, p 25).

OPERATIONAL (TACTICAL) INTELLIGENCE

- At its base level, when a spontaneous situation develops, the assessment of analysis and any judgements made stem very much from the incident being dealt with. In such a situation there is little or no time for anything except a simple information analysis which leads to an action such as making an arrest. From the tactical aspect of operational intelligence, and in a non-spontaneous situation, intelligence can be considered alongside any practical resource to make the best use of it to attain effective outcomes. Operational intelligence is usually utilised fairly quickly. It usually underpins success in specific investigations.

STRATEGIC INTELLIGENCE

- This is a term which generally refers to information that is processed and used to inform longer-term strategies than those required for operational intelligence (Coyne and Bell, 2011). A good example would be the public order implications of a local derby football match that has had problems in the past, and which is scheduled to take place in six months' time. As the fixture approaches, information could be gathered proactively, analysed and used to deploy resources efficiently and effectively at the event.

In both cases, it is beneficial to identify the intelligence requirements of a particular case or event. This is because many sources can be used for information gathering (see Chapter 4) and the key to effective gathering is to identify and retain the focus on what is required and how to obtain it. Such information gathering is linked to an investigation or event from the outset, running alongside the usually greater influx of general information, such as that in Critical thinking activity 1.2 below.

INTELLIGENCE-LED POLICING

This is a term often used by law makers, policy makers and academics and across all levels of policing. Like 'intelligence', there is no single definition of the term. Essentially, it describes the process of gathering information and applying it in a systematic manner to the planning of investigations or inquiries, making decisions to inform strategy or tactics and providing an evidence-based approach to research and scrutinise information (for further reading see *Police Research and Evidence-Based Policing* by Spooner et al, 2022). The concept is that key criminal activities are identified and focused on (sometimes at the expense of other policing tasks). It deals with emerging threats, established policing problems and even horizon scanning, for example the rise of the digital environment within the internet.

All of these intelligence distinctions are now governed by and included within a UK nationally designed structure, the National Intelligence Model (NIM). This is supplemented by the official source for authorised professional (policing) practice (College of Policing, 2022a). Any information gathering must comply with the Human Rights Act 1998 in addition to obeying constraints written into relevant legislation (see Chapter 2). Article 8 of the Act can be summed up as the right to privacy and investigators must show that this has been considered before any action is taken to gather information, use intelligence or take action against an individual.

INFORMATION SECURITY

Information must be treated with respect and handled carefully (see Chapter 2 for laws and regulations). Secure handling of information and intelligence should always be a key element of any training and practice. Computer systems tend to be very well protected in law enforcement, government and business but this does not mean they are invulnerable. The biggest risk to information security is human error, and from time to time you will see in the news that carelessness leads to laptops, other devices and paperwork being left in the back of taxis or train coaches.

- You must always handle information with care and consider its security at all times.

- Never take paperwork home.

- Never copy material onto unsecured flash drives.

- Never work on documents online in an open internet in a public place. Always consider who else may be able to see what you are looking at (physically and virtually).

POLICING SPOTLIGHT

KNOWING THE RISKS

You are tasked with gathering all information held about a series of street robberies involving teenagers and mobile phones. Because there is so much information on the intelligence system, you decide to print it all out and take it home to work on ahead of a deadline in two days' time when your supervisor expects a report. As you put the papers in the back seat of your car, you remember you have a sporting commitment before you go home, after which you will be able to work on the papers for a couple of hours.

- What do you think this spotlight highlights?

- What should your considerations be?

Sample answers are provided at the end of this book.

THE NATIONAL INTELLIGENCE MODEL

Information is currently managed in most UK law enforcement agencies using the National Intelligence Model (NIM). The name is a little misleading because the NIM is also a business model which allows information to be considered as part of a tasking and co-ordinating process. This, in theory, means that information can be used more efficiently to produce outcomes such as arrests, searches and seizures. The idea is that information is quickly processed at a practice level (local intelligence office), subject to fairly immediate decision making by managers (daily tasking and co-ordinating meetings) and acted upon as part of routine policing business (Flood and Gaspar, 2004). It is not a perfect system but it has served the purpose of streamlining what was historically recognised as a disjointed and disparate approach by law enforcement to the gathering and utilisation of information at all levels. Chapter 3 of this book will examine the NIM and its effectiveness in more detail (and Chapter 5, in the section on the intelligence cycle) but as a police officer or other law enforcement investigator using it, some context will be essential for you at this point. Strategic-level governance of force issues and investigations, including the resourcing of them, can effectively feed into the tactical considerations and practical demands of applying them.

The NIM process has three levels of engagement which guide investigators as to the level of criminality under consideration (National Centre for Policing Excellence, 2005a). It is imperative to understand that these three levels are only a guide and that criminality can ascend or descend from one level to another.

- Level 1 – tends to be at local level and is usually dealt with by the police force concerned.

- Level 2 – tends to be on a cross-border level, county to county, and the criminality is more regional than local.

- Level 3 – tends to be serious and organised in its nature. It is criminality which has escalated to a national and international level.

CRITICAL THINKING ACTIVITY 1.2

LEVEL 5

Imagine you have executed a search warrant to recover various items stolen from two shed burglaries in your area. When you enter the premises, you discover the stolen items and uplift them as evidence relating to the crimes you are investigating. While you are lawfully on the premises you find banking information which suggests over one million pounds is in at least seven accounts but only two are in the suspect's name. Two accounts seem to be abroad in Europe. Behind the bath panel you discover over 70 passports in various names, together with blank birth certificates and a book which seems to be a log of sales and payments. You began your day investigating local level 1 criminality; consider the above circumstances and re-apply the NIM levels.

- Has anything changed and why?

- What do you think you should do now?

Sample answers are provided at the end of this book.

INTELLIGENCE TASKING AND CO-ORDINATION

This is a critical part of the current NIM structure whereby information within the system is continually assessed with a view to identifying intervention points (where action can be taken). It is a fairly rapid process if used properly because if information becomes old it should not be used unless it is refreshed and re-checked to see if it remains valid. Tactical tasking and co-ordinating should key into any existing investigation plans as a review function, as well as identifying emerging trends in crime, locally or more widely (in addition to reacting to organic information coming from the public and other such sources) (National Centre for Policing Excellence, 2005a).

Practically speaking, it means that on a day-to-day basis, risks to local policing are fairly effectively identified and dealt with. Incorporated into the decision making at a tactical level is the oversight of resources and how they are allocated to areas of priority. Once tactical options have been considered, agreed upon and recorded, any additional intelligence requirements can be identified before being passed for operational action (College of Policing, 2022a). A very important part of the whole process is a debrief on whatever activity has taken place as a result of acting upon the intelligence produced. This is sometimes a neglected area of policing but, if properly conducted, examines what went well, how effective the action taken was and whether any lessons can be learned.

CRITICAL THINKING ACTIVITY 1.3

LEVEL 6

Imagine you are on foot patrol in the early hours one weekday morning. You are standing in the shadows of a corner shop doorway when you see a yellow BMW motor vehicle pass by. Turning right, next to where you are standing, you see that the driver is John Smith, who you know to have previous convictions for night-time burglaries. You also notice there is a scratch alongside the offside passenger door. As the vehicle pulls away you note down the registration number and note the time as 0405 hours. When you arrive back at the police station towards the end of your shift, you enter what you saw into the computerised intelligence system.

As people start to arrive at work, a burglary and theft is reported at an industrial premises about a mile from where you were standing. There is evidence at the scene that the offence was committed between 0330 and 0400 hours during the night. Yellow paint traces are found on the gate post leading to the rear yard of the building.

- How do you think the information you entered into the intelligence system could be considered and applied by the tasking and co-ordinating meeting that morning?

Sample answers are provided at the end of this book.

POLICE-GENERATED INFORMATION: SURVEILLANCE AND COVERT HUMAN INTELLIGENCE SOURCES

All police forces have the ability to deploy various intrusive tactics to gather information and evidence which require oversight and clear operational guidelines (see Chapter 2 for legal obligations). Such tactics include physical or electronic surveillance of individuals and the handling of informants, now called Covert Human Intelligence Sources (CHIS). These avenues of information gathering are strictly controlled and conducted according to legal oversight (see Chapter 2). Since the Investigatory Powers Act 2016 (see Chapter 2), oversight of how powers are used is also provided by the Investigatory Powers Commissioner's Office (IPCO). This is because, besides police use of investigatory powers, there are over 600 UK public authorities that can use them in some form (IPCO, 2022). The deployment of such tactics is not the focus of this book, and it would not be appropriate to expose police tactics. Instead, this chapter serves as an introduction to the possibilities offered by surveillance and CHIS deployment balanced against the protection of civil liberties.

REFLECTIVE PRACTICE 1.2

LEVEL 4

Imagine that information is received that Jane Doe is responsible for committing a series of high-value robberies at post offices in your area. You are told to follow her until the next robbery is executed, to set up an observation post opposite her known home address and to monitor her emails and social media sites.

- What would your immediate reaction be to these instructions?

- Think about whether you should have that kind of unrestricted power or should such power be regulated? In either case – why?

- What do you think public opinion would be if it was discovered that unregulated and undirected surveillance could be unilaterally used by any police officer and without oversight?

Sample answers are provided at the end of this book.

SURVEILLANCE

Surveillance is defined within the Regulation of Investigatory Powers Act (RIPA) 2000, s.48(2) as the monitoring, observing or listening to persons and their movements, activities and communications (which could include monitoring someone's digital footprint such as social media). By its nature, surveillance is not an overt practice. Anything to do with it falls under covert operations and is dealt with by specialist units. It is usually divided into categories of directed surveillance and intrusive surveillance.

- Directed surveillance – generally speaking this means a *covert* investigation, the purpose of which is to obtain private information about a subject relating to the case or operation.

- Intrusive surveillance – again, this is *covert* and relates to investigative activity in a residential premises of the subject in question or any private vehicle, carried out using a surveillance device (an electronic device deployed by the police to monitor, observe or follow any such activity) (Crown Prosecution Service, 2017). This is something which is authorised only on application to a chief constable or a designated deputy and usually lasts for three months. All authorities must be *necessary* and *proportionate*. These authorities are usually applied for to assist in investigating serious and organised criminality, although they can also be granted for purposes of national security or to protect the economic systems of the UK.

POLICING SPOTLIGHT

Imagine you are a police officer tasked with investigating a series of shop thefts on the town high street. You call in at the various shops and ask each one if they have CCTV footage available for a particular day when the offender is suspected of committing the offences. One shop owner confirms she has such footage but asks you for a surveillance authority in order to hand it over to you.

Think about the definition of directed surveillance and apply it to this situation. You would be quite right to point out that the camera is overt in the store with a notice on the entrance door which states that CCTV operates within the store. On this basis alone, a surveillance authority would not be required. This is underpinned by the fact that the premises is not a residential property or a private vehicle, so intrusive surveillance also does not apply. There may of course be data protection implications to consider (see Chapter 2).

COVERT HUMAN INTELLIGENCE SOURCES

Alongside opportunities to deploy surveillance, the ability to deploy human assets as part of an intelligence-gathering operation is a very important one. Once called informants, CHIS are now the domain of experienced and well-trained police officers who act as CHIS handlers.

The remit of a CHIS is to be *covertly* deployed in a particular situation (usually as a result of the NIM tasking and co-ordination process) to develop relationships and obtain information about an individual, individuals or crime. A CHIS is capable of being tasked, that is, they are there to obtain specific information through observations or listening. CHIS deployments are controlled under the RIPA 2000 legislation and senior oversight is required – usually a superintendent although in certain circumstances it could be an inspector. Authorisation can last for a period of up to 12 months. In the case of juveniles, that period reduces to one month and can only be granted by an officer of the rank of assistant chief constable or above. These are not the only parameters and legislative requirements in place, but the purpose of this chapter is to provide an overview and context to the various aspects of information gathering available to law enforcement. If you would like to read more about RIPA, surveillance and CHIS deployment, a further reading list is at the end of this chapter. It includes a link to the recent legislation under the Covert Human Intelligence Sources (Criminal Conduct) Act 2021.

CRITICAL THINKING ACTIVITY 1.4

LEVEL 5

- Consider the following examples and decide if the individual concerned is a CHIS.

EXAMPLE 1

You are on duty making house-to-house inquiries as a result of a dwelling house burglary and theft the day before. As you are about to get in the car, Mr Smith approaches you and informs you that a teenager called Darren Fox is responsible for the offence. He knows because he saw him force open and enter the side window of the property. Mr Smith is scared of reprisals if he gets involved.

EXAMPLE 2

You are on duty when you are approached by Audrey, who says she is a hairdresser at a nearby salon. Every Friday morning, she has to listen to conversations between two women whose husbands are apparently involved in growing cannabis. Her clients talk quite openly about how much money they have to spend and the various renovations being made to their houses. Audrey works hard and does not see why her clients' husbands should get away with drug trafficking. Audrey provides you her contact details but will not make a formal statement. After liaising with your supervisor, you contact Audrey and ask her if she can find out more details about the husbands of the two women and continue to provide information so that the cannabis, or the money to pay for it, can be located and action taken.

Sample answers are provided at the end of this book.

INFORMATION AND THE INTERNET

This is a relatively new area of policing and investigators face significant challenges when dealing with the digital environment (see Chapter 4). It offers anonymity for offenders, underpinned by the rapidity of information exchange across national and international borders. Most police forces now have so-called cybercrime units, but these are usually small and specialist units. The public, including criminals, have internet access on a 24/7 basis in an area of constantly developing and changing systems, programs, opportunities and access (including smart phones, computers, gaming devices), with many devices now offering an inbuilt opportunity to chat, sometimes with encrypted protection. The police are expected to keep up with this emerging and constantly evolving threat, which is a very difficult proposition for most police forces that are struggling with limited budgets and numbers of staff, most of whom are not trained in this area of intelligence work.

The myth appears to be that criminals routinely access the 'dark web' to conduct their business but this requires expertise, just as it does for law enforcement. In reality, most offences appear to be committed using the top 6 per cent of the internet which we are all familiar with (the world of Google, Amazon, online banking and so on). There is little need for sophistication if you are able to sit in a public library in Brazil and orchestrate a simple global online fraud with little risk of detection or arrest weighed against potentially high rewards. The general use of the internet by criminals now offers possibilities for intelligence gathering by law enforcement.

Policing intelligence efforts tend to revolve around social media sites which not only offer information about offenders but also assist in tracing witnesses, victims or missing persons. The key difference between police and criminal users is the law. Police investigators must adhere to it; criminals do not. An obvious statement perhaps but much of the existing legislation (see Chapter 2) was created to deal with traditional policing problems and has to be 'fitted' to digital issues until a government legislates specifically for the internet environment (the long-awaited Online Safety Bill moving through Parliament). This includes issues around how police obtain information from the internet, how disclosure applies, where limits are reached that then require authority from supervisors and where the jurisdiction of one police force ends (internationally) and another begins (see Chapter 3 for theoretical frameworks). These remain problematic areas for intelligence gathering and investigations (explored in Chapter 4). The following reflective practice exercise explores some of the issues involved in internet intelligence gathering.

REFLECTIVE PRACTICE 1.3

LEVEL 6

Close to the end of your shift, imagine you are asked by a supervisor to begin research on a particular company of interest to an investigation. First of all, you conduct a general search for the company and find it using a well-known search engine. Once on the company website, you 'surf' page to page finding details of directors, photographs of them and the office buildings and information about the trade the business conducts. You then finish for the day knowing the website will be there tomorrow. The following day, you return to the website and print out some material during the morning. As another case interrupts what you are doing, you return to the website in the afternoon to complete your task.

- Do you think you have engaged in surveillance? Explain your answer.

Sample answers are provided at the end of this book.

INTELLIGENCE AND RESEARCH: PARALLELS

It is important to understand that gathering information which can become intelligence is very similar to research you may undertake as a university student. As the government drive is for all police officers to have a recognised qualification in policing (Police Constable Degree Apprenticeship, Degree in Professional Policing or Diploma in Professional Policing Practice), the skills you learn in that qualification process are very important to information gathering as a police officer (see *Police Research and Evidence-Based Policing*, Spooner et al, 2022) regarding how to research a policing project). This section explores the parallels between information gathering for an investigation and any research project you undertake as a police officer, as a student, or in any environment where information is required to produce an output. This is because the essential framework for any information collection to produce an outcome is the same. In either case you will deploy relevant parts of a Six-Step Framework we have developed for when you are gathering information and producing actionable intelligence regardless of the project or investigation.

Six-Step Framework

1. Identify sources.

2. Gather information.

3. Establish the reliability of your sources.

4. Corroborate your sources.

5. Analyse any information you uncover and create actionable intelligence (commonly referred to as the intelligence cycle; see Chapter 5).

6. Utilise the intelligence to identify an intervention point (produce an outcome).

The parallels between information gathering or evidence identification for an investigation and for any research project can be demonstrated by comparing the following two examples.

CRITICAL THINKING ACTIVITY 1.5

LEVEL 6

EXAMPLE 1: INFORMATION OR A DRUNKEN DREAM?

Imagine you are an investigator and have just arrived for duty to be told a man called Brian is in the inquiry office of the police station to see you. The man, Brian, is reported to be drunk and is asking to speak to CID. You take Brian to a witness interview room and he immediately tells you that a woman is dead. Over the next two hours, it becomes clear that he is a chronic alcoholic, and his memory is unreliable. He does not know the woman's name, but she is married to Billy, one of his drinking friends, also an alcoholic. He has never met her but has no reason not to believe that Billy is married. He and Billy had been drinking the night before in the Cat and Pigeon pub in town. During a long day and evening of drinking, Billy started crying. He told Brian that he had been arguing with his wife. This was not unusual but, on this occasion, she would not shut up so Billy had hit her on the head with a claw hammer and killed her. When you have completed a somewhat disjointed and sketchy interview with Brian, he finishes by stating it could have been a dream caused by drink.

You decide that, although Brian's story is possibly an invention of his mind caused by years of alcohol abuse, you had better look into the tale he told.

EXAMPLE 2: THE LEGEND OF THE THREE-TIERED RAM-SHIP

The Winged Ships of Tarsis is a reference to Greek warships called triremes from around 480 BC. They were reputed by ancient historians to have had three tiers of oars and in battle could turn by their own length. They were considered by most later historians to be nothing more than an invention of over-enthusiastic ancient writers. Legend has it that they were the primary instrument in the Battle of Salamis, which destroyed a Persian invasion fleet that year. There appeared to be no physical evidence they existed and could well have been the invention of Greek propaganda writers hundreds of years after the battle. You decide you are going to establish whether they existed or not.

- For Example 1, what do you decide to do and why?

- For Example 2, how will you establish whether triremes existed or not?

- Apply the Six-Step Framework to both examples to help you with a solution.

Sample answers are provided at the end of this book.

It is important to note that the Six-Step Framework is applied to both examples in the same way. In considering the two examples above, you can see that, depending on the nature of the information that you start with, parts of the framework may be more relevant than others. The framework offers flexibility in how you use it.

CONCLUSION

This chapter has provided you with an overview of the information and intelligence-gathering framework currently used by UK policing, signposting on occasion what is to be explored in later chapters. It has explained the difference between information and intelligence, introduced the NIM and how information can broadly be separated into three areas. It has explored police-generated information techniques such as surveillance or CHIS deployment and at all times underpinned the need to check sources and corroborate any information or intelligence before it is used to produce an outcome. Context has been provided for the intelligence potential offered by the digital environment and, finally, comparisons have been presented between investigative information gathering and investigative research, a transferable skill which you can utilise throughout your policing career.

SUMMARY OF KEY CONCEPTS

This chapter has discussed some of the following key concepts.

- Information is not intelligence. Intelligence is the product of a process which analyses the information which has been gathered to produce an outcome – for example, a search warrant or arrest.

- Parallels between information gathering for an investigation and conducting a research project.

- Three levels of the NIM and an introduction to tasking and co-ordination.

- Strategic and tactical intelligence, including surveillance and CHIS handling.

- The Six-Step Framework for gathering information and testing its veracity.

- The difference between directed surveillance and intrusive surveillance.

- The relationship between the internet and intelligence issues for policing.

CHECK YOUR KNOWLEDGE

1. What is the difference between information and intelligence?

2. What are the three main categories of information?

3. What are the three levels of functionality for the NIM framework?

4. What are the component parts of the Six-Step Framework?

5. What do the letters CHIS stand for?

Sample answers are provided at the end of this book.

FURTHER READING

BOOKS AND BOOK CHAPTERS

Grayling, A C (2009) *Liberty in the Great Age of Terror*. St Ives: Clays Ltd.
This is an easy read which weighs up the problems in the police having extensive intrusive powers and the need to protect the rights of the individual.

Spooner, E, Hughes, C and Jones, P (2022) *Police Research and Evidence-Based Policing*. St Albans: Critical Publishing.
A good book that explores the topic of police research and evidence-based policing in detail.

ARTICLES IN JOURNALS

Crous, C (2011) Managing Covert Human Intelligence Sources: Lessons for Police Commanders. *Australasian Policing*, 3(2): 12–15.
This article offers insights into CHIS handling and the constant training required, reviewing examples from the UK, including Northern Ireland, and data collected over six months in Australia.

WEBSITES

College of Policing: www.college.police.uk/app
This website is where all aspects of authorised professional practice for UK policing can be found. It includes sections about surveillance, intelligence and tasking and co-ordination.

CHIS legislation: www.legislation.gov.uk/ukpga/2021/4/contents/enacted
This link is to the Act of Parliament regarding CHIS handling and the accompanying explanatory notes.

CHAPTER 2
LEGISLATION AND INTELLIGENCE GATHERING

LEARNING OBJECTIVES

AFTER READING THIS CHAPTER YOU WILL BE ABLE TO:

- ⚙ understand the necessity for legislation in the United Kingdom to control how information is gathered;

- ⚙ identify the main legislation relevant to the gathering of information;

- ⚙ apply relevant legislative safeguards to information gathering;

- ⚙ balance the rights of the individual against the need to gather information;

- ⚙ enhance intelligence opportunities within the legislative framework by applying available (but little used) powers;

- ⚙ describe the challenges posed by the internet to gathering information using existing legislation.

INTRODUCTION

For in-depth analysis of legislation regarding intelligence, much has been written elsewhere (see the further reading section at the end of the chapter). The aim of this chapter is not to present legal analyses or to compare arguments for or against that legislation. Rather, it is to explore some of the UK legislation governing intelligence handling and to provide context as to how information is gathered, processed and acted upon. It does so by examining some of the practical aspects of how such legislation affects the gathering of information and the impact it may have on you as a police officer. It considers the ethics of intelligence gathering (and handling), and the needs of the state (police and government) to access information weighed against the rights of the individual and the right to privacy (the protections afforded by law). The following critical thinking activity introduces you to Blackstone (1778), the keystone for balancing civil liberties and state power, upon which the majority of legislation is based and designed to protect.

CRITICAL THINKING ACTIVITY 2.1

LEVEL 4

That the whole should protect all its parts and that every part should pay obedience to the will of the whole; or, in other words, that the community should guard the rights of each individual member, and that (in return for this protection) each individual should submit to the laws of the community; without which submission it was impossible that protection could be extended to any.

(Blackstone, 1778)

- What do you think this paragraph is saying about the role and responsibility of the government and the duty of its private citizens?

- Why do you think it is important?

Sample answers are provided at the end of this book.

Think about Blackstone as we examine the main Acts of Parliament relevant to intelligence gathering, including data protection, GDPR implications, Regulation of Investigatory Powers Act 2000, Investigatory Powers Act 2016, Human Rights Act 1998, the anti-terrorist provisions, and other relevant laws pertaining to information/intelligence handling. These central and well-known types of legislation quite rightly govern how intelligence is gathered and used but this chapter also examines less-well-known intelligence pathways created within the legislative framework such as suspicious activity reports (SARs), which can be used to trace victims, witnesses and offenders. Consideration is also given to often little used powers available to the police which can be effectively utilised to enhance intervention opportunities once information has been lawfully gathered (Powers of Criminal Courts (Sentencing) Act 2000). Finally, the chapter considers the implications of the digital environment for information gathering and the current legislation. The internet is stripped down into three parts to demonstrate where information might exist and to consider some of the difficulties which law enforcement might face in retrieving it subject to the legislation introduced in this chapter.

LEGISLATION

Have you ever really considered why we have legislation? Most people don't even think about it, as we all tend to live by a very common-sense approach to life. For instance, we know from a young age that it is wrong to steal, commit other crimes or kill. We are also taught that the police are there to protect us from those wishing to do us harm and that criminals will be brought to justice. What we probably do not consider is how the police operate, what powers they have to gather information and how those powers are used. Whether we are aware of the powers or not, police powers have limits which very often are governed by the same legislation that grants them to protect the public and prevent their abuse, wilful or otherwise. Tables 2.1–2.3 show the main Acts of Parliament which govern intelligence gathering in the UK today, the objective being to provide a practical overview of them.

When considering the legislation in the tables, remember that information is useful at any stage of an investigation, not only in the run up to arrest or prior to court proceedings. The tables are divided between legislation controlling general data handling, legislation which specifically governs police-generated intelligence and legislation which offers potential for taking action in addition to the main investigation powers being used.

Table 2.1 General legislation

Act	Description
Human Rights Act 1998	Incorporated the articles of the European Convention for the Protection of Human Rights and Fundamental Freedoms into UK law. The fundamental points were agreed on by the Council of Europe after the Second World War but were not enshrined into UK law by Parliament until 1998.
Computer Misuse Act 1990	Created offences of unauthorised access to computer material to commit or facilitate an offence, or to commit an act to impair or damage the operation of a computer (eg distributed denial of service attack or ransomware attack). Although updated by the Serious Crime Act 2015 to enable prosecution of anyone supplying equipment to commit computer offences, there is still a need for legislation which will regulate the intelligence aspects of the internet bespoke to the digital environment and to cover things

→

Table 2.1 (*continued*)

Act	Description
	such as accessing social media platforms, piercing internet anonymity and how to deal with the rise of digital assets such as cryptocurrency.
Freedom of Information Act 2000	Made provision for disclosure of information from public bodies on application by any individual. Anyone can request information from a public body, which has to reply within 20 days unless specific circumstances apply such as an ongoing investigation.
General Data Reform Act 2018 and General Data Protection Regulations 2018 (GDPR)	Consolidated and replaced the Data Protection Act 1998. The GDPR created six data protection principles covering how information is obtained, lawfully processed, adequate for purpose, accurate, retained only for as long as necessary and its security maintained. The GDPR applies to all personal information.

Table 2.2 Legislation governing policing methods

Act	Description
Regulation of Investigatory Powers Act 2000	Governs the use of surveillance and electronic surveillance by public bodies, including the use of mobile and static observations and the use of CHIS(s). Regulated **directed surveillance** (observing people, monitoring or listening to communications and deploying CHIS) and **intrusive surveillance** (covert surveillance using eavesdropping devices and which requires authorisation, usually from the Home Secretary).
Terrorism Act 2000	Defined terrorism; created an array of powers including stop and search powers, and other offences such as collecting or recording information to be used to commit an act of terrorism.
Proceeds of Crime Act 2002 (as amended)	Created a regulatory framework for intelligence from financial institutions in the form of suspicious activity reports (SARs) forwarded to the National Crime Agency.
Terrorism Act 2006	Offences created such as attending terrorist training camps, encouraging terrorism, spreading terrorist publications and providing or receiving terrorist training.
Investigatory Powers Act 2016	Regulates the interception of communications and created a new post of Investigatory Powers Commissioner for oversight of the use of powers. Also updated use of powers in the digital environment by preserving internet connection records for the purposes of law enforcement.
Counter-Terrorism and Border Security Act 2019	Updated powers and penalties in the existing Acts as well as providing new offences to deal with offenders who are abroad and advocating acts of terrorism in the UK. Also updated offences to cover material being viewed or streamed over the internet for such purposes.

Table 2.3 Legislation offering additional possibilities for intelligence outcomes

Act	Description
Powers of Criminal Courts (Sentencing) Act 2000	Created powers for courts to use when sentencing individuals for offences. Can be useful in some intelligence cases by allowing a judge in certain circumstances to disqualify an offender from driving and also depriving an offender of a vehicle if used in crime (see Reflective practice 2.2).

All of the above legislation is enacted by Parliament but that does not mean that laws always remain the same. Far from it, as new legislation is usually quickly tested within the UK court system by way of the Court of Appeal. The judiciary becomes the check and balance mechanism to ensure that there is no imbalance in the powers of the state and the rights of the individual and that the law remains fair to all. If the police abuse their powers in one instance, the appeals system ensures the abuse is not repeated. Governments may pass new laws with a specific intent in mind, but the courts have the final say in how the laws can be applied. This is achieved by way of case law (see Spooner et al, 2022).

As a policing student or a new uniformed patrol constable, do you think you need to be aware of the legislation in the tables, most of which might appear at first glance to centre on specialist policing roles such as surveillance units or prevention terrorism? Consider the next reflective practice activity.

REFLECTIVE PRACTICE 2.1

LEVEL 4

PC Brian works as a response car patrol officer in a city centre area. At one of the shift briefings, information is presented to the effect that Simon Simple, a known drug dealer, has moved into a residential address in the area. All officers are shown a photograph of Simon Simple and asked to look out for him. PC Brian has aspirations to become a detective so in an effort to impress the local CID, he uses his initiative and keeps a regular check on the address by driving past it at least three times every shift.

- Do you think PC Brian is doing anything wrong in regularly checking the address?

- Would you do anything differently?

Sample answers are provided at the end of this book.

Even as a routine uniformed patrol officer, there will be times when you need to know what you can and cannot do in an investigation (as shown in the reflective practice example), including how to gather information for your inquiry and the legislation that governs you. The main legislation may well apply to an action you are about to take so always check to see whether there are any protocols or legislative conditions you need to abide by first. Then have a good think about whether the information in front of you can provide additional options for gaining an advantage over a criminal or network and, in the case of a proactive investigation, without necessarily alerting anyone to the fact a wider investigation is being conducted (see Critical thinking activity 2.2 and the next policing spotlight feature for examples).

POWERS

An important part of applying intelligence to ensure real-world outcomes (such as searches and arrests) is not only knowing the primary legislation listed in Table 2.1. It also depends upon the knowledge of powers available to deploy, some of which may be outside usual police thinking or even police training. This is sometimes where traditional police thinking can be slow to change and opportunities to use intelligence effectively can be lost. Although an alternative 'menu of tactics' has now been developed (see Chapter 4), many police officers (including intelligence officers) remain unaware of the 'alternative' powers that can translate what seems to be innocuous information into very effective intelligence. The following critical thinking activity demonstrates how using on-site information can offer alternative possibilities when intelligence seems to confirm police suspicions but then turns out to have a negative result.

CRITICAL THINKING ACTIVITY 2.2

LEVEL 5

Imagine you have been involved in a drug trafficking investigation for two months. The two primary suspects have constantly visited their parents, who live in a disused farmyard with a couple of dwelling houses and large barn. The force helicopter is used to fly over the premises and detects a heat source from one of the outbuildings. Thinking that this is a sure sign of a cannabis grow, the order is given to execute a search warrant at the address. Unfortunately, when the premises are searched, neither of the suspects is present and the room where the heat signature was emanating from is empty. Forensic swabbing of the room reveals no trace of drugs but inside the main dwelling of the farmyard, other officers find large amounts of cash in all rooms. The amount of cash is estimated to be over £250,000. The search co-ordinator is at a loss as to what to do. When you attend the scene after the search warrant has been executed, you notice on arrival that there was a large dog pen along the driveway to the farmhouse. The dogs all seem to be puppies and there are 43 of them in total. You call the RSPCA inspector and ask the occupant of the house if the dogs are pedigree. The householder confirms they are his dogs and that he has been breeding them for ten years. He confirms he does not have a dog breeding licence and nor did he know he required one. You tell the search co-ordinator that a lawful arrest of the householder can now be made for a money laundering offence regarding the cash (nothing at all to do with the drugs warrant).

- Why can you make an arrest and how is the on-site intelligence regarding the dogs relevant (this is not a usual policing device to make an arrest)?

Sample answers are provided at the end of this book.

There are also occasions when the police have all the information that is required to execute a search warrant and make an arrest but they cannot recognise the potential offered by it. It is important to check all the information which is gathered and to be aware that other legislation may help to bring your investigation to a positive conclusion. Sometimes the solution may lie with legislation unfamiliar to you or is not immediately apparent because the potential offence under consideration is not traditionally applied by policing or by the prosecutor. Consider the following policing spotlight to see how actionable intelligence is already held by an investigation team but not immediately recognised.

POLICING SPOTLIGHT

DC Tenor has been assessing information which has been gathered over a three-month period concerning a suspected drug trafficker (of heroin), who is also suspected to be an organiser for a human trafficking crime syndicate. Surveillance tactics have failed on several occasions as the subject never drives his car at more than 40 miles per hour. This would make it fairly obvious if he was being followed and other technical methods have also failed so far to offer intervention opportunities. DC Tenor carefully examines the data gathered from the suspect's eBay account, which had been obtained by a production order (granted by a Crown Court under the Proceeds of Crime Act 2002) at

⟶

the outset of the investigation. It quickly becomes apparent that the suspect owns a gym and has been selling small containers of pills over the internet. Each container has 40 pills, which are marketed as natural steroids to be used when weight training. The ingredients are on the container label. The unit dealing with the investigation has had access to all of this information since the investigation began. DC Tenor simply checks the available information for other possibilities. First of all, she checks with the Health Products Regulatory Authority whether such ingredients are legal to sell and, second, obtains the correct authority for a test purchase to be made under the Regulation of Investigatory Powers Act 2000. The Health Products Regulatory Authority confirms that such pills can only be sold if a licence is obtained because the ingredients constitute a class C drug. The Authority also confirms that no one in the suspect's name or his wife's name has such a licence. When the test purchase sample is examined, forensic tests confirm it to be a class C medicine. DC Tenor recommends that a search warrant be obtained based upon the new information concerning the sale of the pills as well as money laundering the profits, which were totalled to be in excess of £80,000.

This example underpins a very important rule of thumb when dealing with information gathering and the production of intelligence from it:

Always thoroughly check what you have collected so far. It may offer possibilities which have not yet been considered or recognised.

In this example, the information about eBay had been known by the investigation for some months but no one had thought to check the ingredients of the pills and to see if they were being sold legally. The focus of the other officers involved in the case was class A drug supply and people trafficking. It is easy to become focused on one stream of evidence gathering and omit other possibilities. This links to something called an investigative mindset, which means gathering material in a systematic way to underpin an investigation. Effective usage of intelligence involves continuously considering all opportunities presented by the information being gathered and avoiding the pitfall of creating silos that act as inhibitors to wider thinking (in this example, the pills were obviously not heroin and therefore were thought to be irrelevant to the investigation). By taking another approach and checking for different legislation not usually on the police radar, but based upon the same information, a practical outcome was achieved. Consider the next reflective practice activity to see how integrating information and knowledge of available powers can also contribute to a better practical outcome.

REFLECTIVE PRACTICE 2.2

LEVEL 5

Imagine you are a police officer on a Safer Neighbourhood Team. You are aware that a recent domestic at an address in your area caused actual bodily harm to a woman at the premises. Her estranged husband had driven from another county in his car, pulled up outside the house and punched her hard in the face when she answered the door. She sustained injuries of a black eye and a cut to the side of the head. While on general patrol, you are told by a neighbour that the man will come back after the court case is over and probably commit similar offences.

- If a court case is already going ahead regarding the initial assault, what else might be done here regarding the new information from the neighbour?

Sample answers are provided at the end of this book.

SUSPICIOUS ACTIVITY REPORTS

Certain systems within the business sector are in place so that information can be securely passed to law enforcement. One of these which you, as a general patrol officer, can tap into is a suspicious activity report (SAR). Any financial institution in the UK which suspects that a transaction is suspicious must report that transaction by way of a SAR to the National Crime Agency. This is not a choice. It is a matter of law, under section 330 of the Proceeds of Crime Act 2002. SARs are generally thought to be the remit of financial investigators and due to this misperception are generally unused by general patrol officers. They have been included separately in this chapter because they can be extremely useful for patrol officers to locate not only suspects but also witnesses or victims of crime. This is because they can contain useful information such as:

- date of birth;

- current address;

- email details;

- National Insurance number (sometimes);

- associated addresses;

- associate names;

- business connections.

The main issue is that most police officers do not know what a SAR is, what information can be offered in a SAR or where to access it. The simple answer is that most intelligence units now have access to SARs as well as financial investigation units, some of which are now based within policing divisions rather than being isolated at police headquarters.

A word of caution though. Do not expect to be given a SAR to walk away with. They are 'owned' by the National Crime Agency and classed as restricted documents because they are received directly from the financial institutions. Because of this, SARs are usually not openly visible for general perusal on intelligence systems, but most forces use a unique reference system which allocates a number. If you are part of a police force which uses such a system or not, just visit the financial investigation office or an intelligence office and you should be able to gain access to the information.

ETHICS OF INTELLIGENCE GATHERING

Human rights legislation in the UK demands that investigations are proportionate in the powers being used, in particular Article 8, which is the individual's right to privacy. Article 3 prevents torture and Article 6 protects the right to a fair trial (since the Criminal Procedure and Investigations Act 1996 was passed, law enforcement have been held accountable for all documentation, including intelligence, connected to any investigation). Despite these articles, why should you be concerned about how you gather intelligence? Surely the end justifies the means so if what you do results in an arrest, why would anyone care how you achieved your goal? This links to what is termed noble cause corruption – bending the rules for a greater good. This is something you should avoid doing as bending the rules is arguably corrupt as a concept.

EVIDENCE-BASED POLICING

HUMAN RIGHTS ACT 1998: ARTICLE 8

When you gather information either as an intelligence specialist or as an investigator, Article 8 of the Human Rights Act must always be considered. It clearly states: '*Everyone has the right to respect for his private and family life, his home and his correspondence*' (Human Rights Act 1998). These rights can only be breached by law enforcement for reasons of national security, or public safety (such as the prevention of disorder or crime), to protect the rights and freedoms of others or to protect general health or morals.

What this means in concise terms is that any person in the UK has the right to live their life without government interference except in the instances outlined. Think about the legislation outlined in this chapter and notice that as a police officer you will have to apply for authority to conduct surveillance of any kind. This is because you need to show to either a senior supervisor or a court the fact that you have considered Article 8 and can explain the rationale for the action you want to take. If you cannot do so, then your course of action should not be authorised. Think about how you would react if your emails and communications were unprotected and could be viewed at any time by law enforcement or government without cause or reason. The laws in Tables 2.1, 2.2 and 2.3 are a protection against such unjustified intrusion.

The basic point is that a police officer has to work within the law, while the offender always has an advantage in that criminal activity has no boundaries and is outside the law (remember Blackstone). You need clear reasons for your intended actions and inquiries. No matter how dire the situation or how desperate you may be to obtain information, you must always do so lawfully. The actions of a police officer are expected to always be transparent and ethical. Consider the next critical thinking activity and assess the example provided.

CRITICAL THINKING ACTIVITY 2.3

LEVEL 6

Imagine you have arrested a husband and wife shop theft team and during the course of interviewing them for the alleged offences you are approached by a member of your major crime unit, who informs you that the man is a close friend of someone who is currently the target of a multiple robbery investigation. You are asked to speak to the man and get his co-operation to become an informant (a Covert Human Intelligence Source) and provide information which can lead to the arrest of his friend. If the man refuses to engage with the idea, you are instructed to inform him that if he complies with the request, then no charges will be brought against his wife for the various shop theft offences she has been arrested for.

- What will your course of action be and why?

Sample answers are provided at the end of this book.

There is always an ethical debate as to how information is obtained and in the wake of the existing terrorist threat, the debate has perhaps never been so relevant. Consider Guantanamo Bay, for example, the terrorist prison compound used by the US Security Services based outside the reach of US jurisdiction (courts, law enforcement and civil rights). It is a fact that inmates at the facility are in effect tortured for information. The most well-known torture applied is 'waterboarding', where a suspect is almost drowned repeatedly in an attempt to gain information. The US government appears to feel that this is a legitimate form of questioning. In academic terms it is known as the consequentialist approach – Richards (2010, p 89) acknowledges former US Defence Secretary Dick Cheney's assertion that torture can be shown to work sometimes and explores the ethical issues such a view presents. However, most countries and commentators accept that torture does not work well in principle, and in the UK the Human Rights Act 1998 prohibits its use. Unlike the UK, the United States has not implemented any human rights legislation. This raises questions surrounding the exchange of intelligence with countries performing or allowing acts of torture. UK police cannot use information to prosecute offenders if it was obtained abroad using torture in any form, whether mental or physical. Information or so-called evidence of terrorism or other criminal activity cannot be relied upon or used to prosecute anyone in the UK court system.

Despite US (and other) claims that torture occasionally works, the central problem outside of the human rights debate is whether information extracted under torture can be relied upon. Many confessions or information extractions are made simply because the person subject to the torture wants it to stop and will tell the interrogator anything to that end. It is interesting to note that in the UK we use the term 'interviewing a suspect' (or witness) in order to obtain an account of what has happened. The Americans refer to the same process as interrogation, a process to gain a confession.

Torture is perhaps an extreme example of the importance attached to ethical behaviour when information gathering. The principle applies at all levels of policing. Consider the following critical thinking activity.

CRITICAL THINKING ACTIVITY 2.4

LEVEL 6

You are dealing with a prisoner who has been arrested on suspicion of burglary. There is very little forensic evidence available, and you know that it is likely there will be no offence charged. While the custody officer is dealing with the release of your prisoner, you covertly carve a three-centimetre line in the sole of their right shoe. Three days later, the same man is arrested again but, on this occasion, it can be proven that the shoes he is wearing on arrest forensically match the footprints left at the scene of the burglary.

- Consider the legislation in Tables 2.1 and 2.2. By your actions you have generated usable intelligence but have you acted appropriately, ethically and lawfully in this situation? Explain your answers.

Sample answers are provided at the end of this book.

INTERNET INTELLIGENCE

Police officer familiarity with the internet environment is often not uniform and usually depends on an individual's personal digital expertise. The internet has added a completely new dimension to policing and the gathering of information. Social media platforms in particular offer a wealth of information, not only about criminals, their associates and connected businesses, but also about witnesses and victims. Platforms such as WhatsApp, Twitter, LinkedIn, TikTok and Facebook are just a few of the more well-known sites from which information can be harvested. There are of course a myriad of others. Boundaries within cyberspace are not obvious and criminals can utilise its seeming capacity for anonymity to great effect. It is not quite that simple, however, because like the police criminals also need a degree of expertise if the internet is to be used to their advantage and with intentional complexities to make it difficult for law enforcement to follow their activities. Their main advantage is that they have no legal boundaries to worry about and, unlike the real world, the internet has no local, regional or international boundaries once it is accessed.

There is a presumption that all people are now familiar with how the internet operates, usually based on the mistaken premise that we all use it. This section breaks cyberspace down into three areas.

1. **The surface web.** This is the general internet in which Google, Amazon and a myriad of businesses exist (including the financial industry) and conduct their trade.

2. **The deep web.** The place where the systems for businesses to conduct their trade are embedded.

3. **The dark web** (sometimes known as Onion sites). The place where nefarious activities take place in a largely anonymous environment which functions on a unique road map system of blocks. It is not only a place for criminals to conduct illegal activities; it also serves other functions such as allowing political dissident voices to get their messages out to democratic countries when their own countries are subject to martial law or where citizens are denied the freedom of speech (such as in Russia or China).

The problem for law enforcement is that without specialist training, police officers find it extremely difficult to access anything other than the surface web for information. Most internet-related investigations are conducted by cyber units, but these tend not to be staffed in large numbers. Their investigations (including intelligence gathering) are not straightforward because, unlike criminals, police investigators not only have to work within the law but have to investigate using legislation which is unable to keep pace with the way the digital environment has expanded.

The Computer Misuse Act 1990 was written at a time when the internet was in its infancy and aside from amendments or additions such as in the Serious Crime Act 2015, there is no specific legislation which clarifies exactly what is or is not lawful for investigators when searching the digital environment for information. The Acts mentioned in Table 2.1 are relied on for guidance. The Online Safety Bill currently passing through the House of Lords at the Committee Stage may alter or add to laws currently used to investigate digital offending. Consider the next critical thinking activity.

CRITICAL THINKING ACTIVITY 2.5

LEVEL 6

Imagine PC Smithson is investigating a romance fraud allegation (where a criminal deliberately baits another individual (male or female) into an online electronic relationship which, over time, is used to extort money from the victim). In an attempt to catch the criminal, PC Smithson creates a false identity online and accesses the site thought to be used to attract victims. She enters into a long-running conversation with someone who appears to be a fraudster. The intention is that by using bogus photographs and personal details, PC Smithson will effectively set the bait to eventually entice the criminal into a situation where an arrest can be made.

- Examine PC Smithson's actions. Are they lawful or unlawful and why?

- Are there any other considerations which you would apply to this type of online investigation?

Sample answers are provided at the end of this book.

CONCLUSION

This chapter has introduced you to the main legislation which governs the use of police powers applied to information gathering in the real world and the internet. The intricacies of legislation are discussed in abundance elsewhere and the point of this chapter was to present an overview of the existing legislation (Tables 2.1 and 2.2) but then apply it to practical scenarios you are likely to become involved in if you pursue a career as a police officer. The practical examples provided in this chapter are all real inquiries or situations and should provide a springboard for further reading or considerations as you think about information and intelligence, and, more importantly, how you understand it has to be gathered. Central to all of the themes discussed is the underlying 'holy grail' of information gathering. The rights of any individual must be respected, and interference from the state (law enforcement) must be necessary, proportionate and legal.

SUMMARY OF KEY CONCEPTS

This chapter has discussed some of the following key concepts.

- Blackstone (1778) and the concept of state power balanced against individual rights.

- Thoroughly checking the information you collect from all aspects, not just the main avenue of inquiry.

- Knowledge of powers offered by different legislation can offer intervention opportunities when traditional investigative avenues are unsuccessful.

- Considering which legislation may be pertinent from the outset of an investigation and what permissions may be required if police-generated intelligence is required.

- Human rights legislation is not an inhibitor to policing. It is there to protect you as the investigator as well as the general public by ensuring that no government oversteps the line between legislating for and using appropriate powers and creating legislation which rides roughshod over individual rights (the so-called Big Brother state where, for example, all private communications could be monitored without having a reason to do so).

- The internet offers new avenues of information which are accessible 24 hours a day, but investigators must still work within the legislative parameters. The fact that access is so easy does not negate the right to privacy or the need to apply for relevant permissions concerning surveillance of internet sites, social media or interception of communications.

- All information gathering is subject to ethical considerations as well as legislative safeguards, in particular Article 8 of the Human Rights Act 1998.

CHECK YOUR KNOWLEDGE

1. Name the main piece of legislation which governs the use of police surveillance.

2. What is the name of the Act which for certain offences allows suspects to be disqualified from driving after their prison sentence?

3. Why are ethics important in information gathering and any intelligence outcomes?

4. What information can be included in a suspicious activity report (SAR)?

5. Name the three sections of the internet.

6. What is the name of the legislation which applies to how computers are used?

Sample answers are provided at the end of this book.

FURTHER READING

BOOKS AND BOOK CHAPTERS

McKay, S (2018) *Blackstone's Guide to the Investigatory Powers Act 2016.* Oxford: Oxford University Press.
This is a good book that explores the topic of the Investigatory Powers Act and the updates to the RIPA legislation.

ARTICLES IN JOURNALS

Egawhary, E M (2019) The Surveillance Dimensions of the Use of Social Media by UK Police Forces. *Surveillance and Society,* 17(1/2): 89–104. [online] Available at: https://ojs.library.queensu.ca/index.php/surveillance-and-society/article/view/12916/8481 (accessed 3 February 2023).
This article explores how UK police forces use social media to gather information and the legalities of doing so and is itself based upon freedom of information requests to those police forces.

Fussey, P and Sandhu, A (2020) Surveillance Arbitration in the Era of Digital Policing. *Theoretical Criminology*, 26(1): 3–22.
This article will help you think about the difficulties of applying existing legislation to the new digital internet environment and so-called surveillance arbitration (where old laws are made to fit new circumstances).

WEBSITES

Citizens Advice: www.citizensadvice.org.uk/law-and-courts/civil-rights/human-rights/what-rights-are-protected-under-the-human-rights-act

Crown Prosecution Service guidance on the Computer Misuse Act 1990 (as amended): www.cps.gov.uk/legal-guidance/computer-misuse-act

Crown Prosecution Service guidance on surveillance authorisations: www.cps.gov.uk/legal-guidance/disclosure-manual-chapter-26-dealing-surveillance-authorisations

CHAPTER 3
INTELLIGENCE-LED POLICING AND THE NATIONAL INTELLIGENCE MODEL

LEARNING OBJECTIVES

AFTER READING THIS CHAPTER YOU WILL BE ABLE TO:

- understand the concept of intelligence-led policing;

- identify the key areas of the National Intelligence Model (NIM);

- apply the three levels of criminality within the NIM to operational matters;

- recognise why information needs to be sanitised;

- understand the system of information governance using the government-designed security classification system;

- make an assessment of information and extract salient points to develop intelligence and intervention points.

INTRODUCTION

As a student exploring the intelligence world for the first time, the wealth of information made available by successive governments, academia and external commentators (including the media, documentaries and think tanks such as the Royal United Services Institute, RUSI), and the spectrum of law enforcement may appear quite daunting. Much of the literature considers theoretical aspects of intelligence and intelligence-led policing, together with the overall effectiveness of systems such as the National Intelligence Model (NIM). With so much reading available, the aim of this chapter is more practically oriented to demonstrate how information should be sanitised, how intelligence items should be compiled and how the NIM is applied within the policing environment. It contextualises the concept of intelligence-led policing and examines the impact of the digital environment on intelligence potential, as well as how information is collected, developed and disseminated using the NIM. The NIM will be considered as a business and decision-making model, focusing on how it works and how information is processed. You may recognise the famous case in the following policing spotlight.

POLICING SPOTLIGHT

THE YORKSHIRE RIPPER INVESTIGATION 1975–1980

This investigation failed to prevent the murders of 13 women in the north of England and has become renowned for its intelligence failures. Although the investigation took place in a world prior to the digital age, it demonstrates some of the key pitfalls when gathering information. After a post-investigation inquiry, a report was issued by Sir Lawrence Byford (1981), which identified a litany of policing failures including attitudes to victims and inept intelligence analysis that probably led to the murder of more victims (Peter Sutcliffe could have been apprehended sooner and by targeted policing as opposed to accidental circumstances). Here are some of the observations in the Byford Report:

*   too much information and no real way to properly analyse it (a card index system was used at the time);

*   limited cross-referencing of the information gathered during the investigation (if this had taken place, officers would have noticed that Peter Sutcliffe's car had been seen 60 times in various red-light districts where victims were abducted or killed);

- much of the information remained unprocessed for months or years;

- hoax letters and tape recordings allegedly from the offender were allowed to derail the main investigation and other lines of inquiry were halted or significantly delayed;

- victims who were not sex workers were disregarded (six victims were not sex workers and information and evidence was lost).

The Ripper case is perhaps one of the key watershed moments for UK policing because, for the first time, policing failings regarding intelligence and a major criminal inquiry were identified and published in a comprehensive report which the government of the day could not ignore. The underlying points then and now remain the same.

- Too much information can inhibit good investigation.

- All information gathered for an inquiry needs to be examined and cross-referenced (this was made easier with the advent of technology but is essential in every case).

- A system is required for considering information and deciding on its relevance and potential for outcomes.

- Information must be objectively assessed, and all forms of bias eliminated from the analysis process.

- The source and integrity of information must always be checked and verified and the information needs to be corroborated.

- Information is only as good as it is effectively used and applied.

Regarding the aspects noted in this policing spotlight, in this chapter elements of the intelligence system are explored in more detail such as the allocation of resources, tactical assessment, tasking and co-ordinating and developing intervention points (practical outcomes). The 3x5 intelligence system is explained, together with why information may need to be sanitised, why information needs to be checked and verified (re-enforcing the initial information discussed in Chapter 1) and how information is governed by a Government Security Classification system (including source evaluation, classification and an assessment of the information being submitted). This chapter encourages the reader to understand that intelligence is a core function within modern-day policing before moving on in the next chapter to recognise the intelligence theatres available for routine and specialist policing.

WHAT IS INTELLIGENCE-LED POLICING?

Intelligence-led policing appears to be defined differently depending on the country you are in. In the UK, it was (and remains) a term originally applied to describe an approach to reducing crime that moved away from reactive (retrospective) investigations towards those based upon analysed information (intelligence) (House of Lords, 2008). Policing was gradually coming around to the idea that instead of waiting for crimes to occur and then having to deal with them, it was possible in many cases to begin a covert investigation and generate information using a variety of methods (see Chapter 4) to dismantle criminal organisations, businesses and individuals ensconced in criminal activity. Such an approach meant the need for a standardised intelligence handling system, better use of police resources and a clear and transparent decision-making model. Due to there being 43 separate police forces in the UK, change was forged in policing under The Police Reform Act 2002 and a subsequent Code of Practice for the new National Intelligence Model (NIM). These provided the statutory basis for the introduction of the NIM minimum standards in the UK while at the same time across Europe, the European Criminal Intelligence Model was adopted based upon the NIM. Intelligence-led policing, as it remains today, became the common working method for the European Union (House of Lords, 2008). The NIM is discussed in more detail later in the chapter.

Now consider the two case examples in the following critical thinking activity.

CRITICAL THINKING ACTIVITY 3.1

LEVEL 4

1. Imagine you are a police officer and arrive at work for a morning shift. On your desk is information received during the night that a woman who lives in a residential property in your area has possession of a quantity of generators stolen from building sites in recent months. The address is 123 ABC Street. The woman is thought to be called Jade.

2. You arrive at work to be told by your sergeant that two men have been arrested for an offence of dwelling house burglary during the night. Officers on the night shift have completed witness statements and obtained statements from a neighbour who saw the two men break into the building and can identify

them both. A crime scene investigator has attended the scene and obtained fingerprint evidence and blood from a broken window. One of the offenders has a three-centimetre cut on his left hand. The other man was searched on arrest and was found to be in possession of a small crowbar with paint flakes which match the colour of the back door of the house where it appears that an unsuccessful attempt was made to force it open. Searches have been conducted at both suspects' addresses and nothing further has been found.

- Consider each example. Does either fit an example of intelligence-led policing? What are the reasons for your answer?

Sample answers are provided at the end of this book.

Terminology applied to intelligence-led policing can sometimes be confusing. The following terms explained in Table 3.1 and based upon the current authorised professional practice from the College of Policing (2022c) explain the four product areas within the NIM.

Table 3.1 Terminology explained

Term	Explanation
Strategic assessment	Used to draw inferences of current or longer-term issues and make recommendations. It can involve partner agencies and requires collection and analysis of information on an ongoing basis concerning identification of key threats and emerging issues.
Tactical assessment	Identifies issues for consideration by a tasking and co-ordination group, which at a divisional level usually meets daily to identify immediate problems, review intelligence requirements and consider any emerging trends. The wider the attendance usually means better analysis of available information and any outcomes arising.
Subject profile	These contain information to assist in the investigation of an individual but at the same time record the rationale for any tasks or actions to identify and fill any intelligence gaps. The rationale for investigation and any tactics deployed in investigating an individual must comply with the Human Rights Act 1998 (see Chapter 2).
Problem profile	These can consider crime trends, identify prevention opportunities and record justification of any action taken. Information should be carefully considered (at all stages), new sources identified and any recommendations recorded.

These areas seem straightforward but can become quite complicated in more complex investigations. Strategic and tactical assessments are usually the domain of supervisors or intelligence specialists but in terms of routine policing a subject profile is useful at any level of inquiry. The more information you have about an individual or business, the less room for errors in police practice. At the same time, a subject profile will also consider the rationale and proportionality of an inquiry, including taking account of human rights implications while compiling it.

REFLECTIVE PRACTICE 3.1

LEVEL 5

Mabel Landsbury, aged 79, lives at 41 Bread and Butter Street. Over the last few weeks she has been constantly woken up in the middle of the night by 'comings and goings' next door at number 39. She dare not approach the resident (Matthew Joby) of the address to complain because she once mentioned his two Doberman dogs barking at night-time and he kicked her fence panels down. She has seen parcels being delivered to the address and then an hour later a stream of people start to arrive, stay for a few minutes and then leave. She was outside her front gate after returning from shopping one day last week when Joby arrived with what seemed to be a large bag of cash. He saw her watching and stuck two fingers up at her. She later looked out of her rear bedroom window and could see Joby burying what appeared to be bundles of cash wrapped in clingfilm under the floor of his ferret pen.

- Have a go at writing the intelligence you would like to submit for this information.

- Then read the NIM paragraphs to see if you have completed your intelligence submission correctly. How did you do?

Sample answers are provided at the end of this book.

IMPACT OF THE DIGITAL ENVIRONMENT ON INTELLIGENCE GATHERING

Before considering the NIM in a little more detail and its role in intelligence work, we need first to consider the impact that the constantly emerging digital environment has had on policing and the infrastructure in place to handle information and the production of intelligence. Chapter 2 provided some context for the internet and how accessing information is governed by various Acts of Parliament, while this chapter will consider how policing has adapted to new information (and offending) opportunities.

The initial point is the 24-hour, seven-days-a-week access the internet affords to everyone. Modern life seems dependent upon it and though it is becoming regarded as a treasure trove of information for law enforcement to access, the potential for criminal activity seems unlimited as it can be anonymous or encrypted. An array of criminality can take place using the digital environment, for example:

- sex offending;

- paedophilia;

- human trafficking recruitment and arrangements;

- money laundering;

- terrorist propaganda;

- terrorist recruitment;

- trading in illegal armaments;

- fraud;

- identity theft;

- cyber attacks;

- hacking;

- Distributed Denial of Service attacks (DDOS).

Other activities such as cyber stalking, cyber bullying, spoof sites, misinformation sites (fake news) and many more are not covered by specific legislation in many countries including the UK and remain problematic for policing on an international level. Sometimes new thinking is required based on existing legislation which can allow investigators to level the playing field against criminals in certain circumstances. Check out the real-life case in the next evidence-based policing example to see how the internet can be used to an investigator's advantage.

EVIDENCE-BASED POLICING

A man was suspected of being a professional enabler for an organised crime group (someone such as a corrupt solicitor, accountant, stock-broker or estate agent, for example) and appeared to run a legitimate business within the financial sector. Rather than take a risk and obtain a search warrant which could prove negative, it was proving difficult for the investigation team to gather information which would lead to an arrest where there would be a positive result at the time of the search and where, in effect, the enabler would be caught red-handed. If a search warrant proved negative then the police investigation would have been exposed to the suspected enabler and the organised crime group, wasting months of intelligence and investigation work. Various bank accounts (personal and business) had been identified for this individual and these were passed to the financial investigation unit to examine. It quickly became apparent that the enabler conducted business online and from home every second Friday and was always online between 10am and noon. The Proceeds of Crime Act 2002 created an investigation tool called an account monitoring order (AMO) and it was suggested one be used for this investigation. An AMO is obtained from a Crown Court and orders a financial institution (in this case a bank) to provide real-time intelligence in respect of an individual or business for up to 90 days in the future. The application needs to be proportionate so in this case the initial order was for 21 days as it was every two weeks that the enabler was known to be online from his account records. A search warrant was obtained and on the following Friday the AMO allowed the financial institution to alert the police that the enabler was online in an account suspected to be used for money laundering. The search team entered the home address by force so as not to alert the enabler and captured him actually online in the account which was being used to move criminal money. At the address a large amount of cash was also seized (over £400,000).

This remains an excellent example of intelligence-led policing based upon previous information and using existing legislative powers in a new and digitally compliant way. It provides a legal and effective advantage to law enforcement in the way that information can be used to transform digital information into a practical outcome.

One of the very real problems is the speed at which criminals can conduct their business and across as many international boundaries as they want in the same day. Although some information may be obtained through internet interrogation, the reality is that to prosecute offenders, law enforcement authorities require reliable information which can lead to real-world interventions (such as searches, recovery of property, arrests). Remember as well, from Chapter 2, that police forces must operate within the law, which means the speed at which criminals can commit offences cannot be matched by investigation.

The key for law enforcement is that once information is created, no matter what its form within the internet, there will be a record of it somewhere. That means, despite the practical and physical difficulties presented by cyberspace, there is information to find, intelligence to be created and results to be obtained.

Practically speaking, you may be able to access information through an intelligence office or cybercrime unit depending upon the nature of your investigation or hunt for information. Remember the legal limitations explained in Chapter 2 and the best advice is to contact your nearest intelligence or cybercrime office, depending on the nature of the information you require.

THE NATIONAL INTELLIGENCE MODEL

The NIM was designed to fulfil a need to standardise information being handled by police and other law enforcement agencies. When information is entered into the NIM, it should as far as possible already have been checked or corroborated. Any risk to the source of the information will always be the responsibility of the organisation in which the information is handled. As part of a standardised system, the submitted report or document should never reveal details of the source of the information and this applies to police officers as well as members of the public. All 43 police forces (and other law enforcement agencies) in the UK use the NIM to manage intelligence and tasking and co-ordinating procedures. There are two points to note.

1. This does not mean police forces act in exactly the same way, but the point is that there is only one intelligence model being used. If you work in Southampton or Northumbria, the model remains the same although forms and protocols may vary slightly.

2. It does not mean that police forces can all interrogate each other's information. They are not linked and are subject to the data protection legislation, as explained in Chapter 2.

Any information entered into the NIM in any police force is allocated a unique reference number so that it can be easily located. It should then be assessed by an intelligence officer before being considered at a tasking and co-ordinating meeting if there is the possibility of an intervention point (an opportunity to take action). Much has been and no doubt will continue to be written about the NIM and its effectiveness as a business model for dealing with information and intelligence. In practice, there are five practical stages required within each of the sections considered in Table 3.1:

1. gathering of information;

2. analysis of information;

3. decision making at a strategic or tactical level (tasking and co-ordination);

4. planning and resources allocation;

5. operational execution.

You can remember these five parts using the mnemonic GADPO. They apply to all three levels of criminality within the NIM (see Chapter 2).

TASKING AND CO-ORDINATION

The NIM is designed as a business model which has the flexibility for information to be inputted, considered and acted upon relatively quickly. This is accomplished by using tasking and co-ordinating (T&C) meetings where information can be turned into action and resources allocated at the level required. T&C meetings can be held as part of a strategic, tactical or practice level. The objective is the same at any level within the NIM: to support operational decision making. Consider the next critical thinking activity.

CRITICAL THINKING ACTIVITY 3.2

LEVEL 5

Information has been inputted into the intelligence system in your police area and you are present in the tactical-level T&C meeting. The information being discussed is as follows.

John Jones is suspected of drug dealing. Information has been received from an informant (a Covert Human Intelligence Source) to the effect that John Jones is importing 20 kilos of cocaine every three months. He uses either Dover or Southampton ports to ship in part of the commodity.

Close associates are described as Desmond Smith of 123 Despatchio Street, Manchester and Cassie Murdoch of 456 Swann Avenue, Manchester. Cassie's mother lives in Cheltenham, and is a previous drug user. John Jones is believed to possess a section 1 firearm – a revolver – no other details known.

- Imagine you attended the T&C meeting to discuss this information. What do you think your main considerations would be?

Sample answers are provided at the end of this book.

SUBMITTING AN INTELLIGENCE ITEM

If you become a police officer and find yourself compiling an intelligence item for submission into the NIM within your area, there are three source gradings:

1. reliable;

2. untested;

3. not reliable.

These are matched against an intelligence assessment grading matrix which has five parts, A to E. These are presented in Table 3.2 in simplified form and are based upon the available College of Policing (2022a) information.

Table 3.2 Intelligence gradings

Grading	What it means
A	Indicates information which is known directly by the source. For example, if a police officer observes something or discovers information, the officer would be the source. If it is a member of the public, then that person would be the source. If the information is from a CHIS, the CHIS would the source. This grading does not include anything which is not personally known to the source of the information. Third-party information or gossip cannot be included here.

$\longrightarrow$

Table 3.2 (*continued*)

Grading	What it means
B	This is for information which is offered by a source but not something which the source has directly observed or experienced. Any information under this grading would require corroboration of some sort. Corroboration should not be from the same source or related to it. For example, a person working in an investment bank overhears a conversation that a member of the company is involved in insider trading of shares. The person passes the information to the police. In this example, the information is not known directly by the source. The person has not witnessed shares being illegally traded. Unlike grading A, the information is not directly known by the source. However, it is something which could be corroborated by various checks within the business systems, on the stock exchange or in the suspect's share portfolio. Corroboration would therefore be independent of the source of the information.
C	Information which technically in a court would be called 'hearsay' falls into this category. It represents information which a source has been informed of by someone else. As an example, imagine you are on duty and a woman approaches you to tell you that she has heard that a man called Smithy King is responsible for breaking into garden sheds in the area, stealing gardening equipment and selling it at an open market stall in the adjacent county. All of this information is third hand but parts of it are capable of being corroborated.
D	This classification is for information which cannot be (easily) assessed. An example would be where the force communications room receives an anonymous call with information that a local man, Jimmy Smith (not known on police records), is responsible for downloading films from a streaming service and selling them on the black market.
E	Information suspected of being false or deliberately misleading is in this category. An example would be where a wife has separated from her husband and continues to maliciously provide false information about the husband being a criminal in order to influence a court case for custody of their three children.

All five assessment gradings demonstrate why it is essential to determine the provenance of information as far as possible before it is submitted into the NIM. T&C meetings need to consider accurate information and the 3x5 system is a standardisation tool to ensure parity in the way intelligence is handled within the 43 separate police forces and other law enforcement agencies. It also makes training police officers much simpler. No matter which police force you join, the intelligence assessment criteria will be the same everywhere.

REFLECTIVE PRACTICE 3.2

LEVEL 4

When compiling an intelligence item for submission into the NIM, remember to be clear and concise. Make certain there is no way that the source of the information can be identified from what you have written. Carefully consider the intelligence grade you are recording the information against. Before submitting the item remember to corroborate the information from other sources if applicable.

- Try sanitising the following information for submission into the NIM.

  Information has been received from a covert human intelligence source that a white male called Colin is dealing drugs from a vacant house at 123 ABC Street. He attended a party on Thursday night last week and when drunk, revealed to those present that he is supposed to be fetching a quantity of drugs from Manchester on Friday next week. He will likely be using a red Datsun motor car registered number COL 1N.

- What steps would you take to provenance the information that has been provided?

Remember not to talk about specific police intelligence items in general conversations, even with other police officers. It is usually not necessary to do so, and the old Second World War truism holds true: '*Walls have ears*'.

Sample answers are provided at the end of this book.

ASSESSING INFORMATION

A myriad of information is reported to the police on an hourly basis and there is far too much data involved for the police to action every piece of it. Many entries into the NIM are very straightforward and routine policing examples tend to be sightings, other observations made while on patrol or information from members of the public regarding everyday low-level offending. Intelligence officers and other investigators are trained to look at the information that has been submitted and to identify the possible courses of action arising from it. Consider the following critical thinking activity.

CRITICAL THINKING ACTIVITY 3.3

LEVEL 6

Imagine you are a police officer and have been placed on secondment to the intelligence unit of a regional organised crime unit (ROCU). You are tasked with sifting information received in the last few days and notice the following letter.

To whom it may concern.

I am writing to inform you that Jean Kevlar, the Chief Executive Officer of Defence Industries Limited, is paying off government officials in Afghanistan and Iraq so that she can ensure continued orders for her company and its subsidiaries.

In the last 18 months she has managed to secretly buy enough shares in her main opposition company, Fighting Accessories Limited, to allow her to appoint two company directors on its board. Those two directors have now set up an offshore account in the Isle of Man in the same company name. They have begun to fraudulently syphon off funds from the cash-rich arm of Fighting Accessories Limited, a subsidiary company called Protective Vests for Theatres of War (UK) Limited.

I suggest that all of this should be investigated right away. As an incentive please be aware that I will be watching and waiting to see justice is done.

- What intelligence grading would you put on this information?

- How can you begin to corroborate the information in the letter?

- What lines of inquiry can you consider?

Remember that all intelligence entered into the NIM uses the same 3x5 system.

Sample answers are provided at the end of this book.

SANITISING INFORMATION

On many occasions, members of the public provide information to the police but do not want to provide a witness statement or become involved in a court case. Any information provided on this basis still needs to be entered into the police intelligence system but with great care. An individual cannot be forced to provide a statement to the police regarding any information being provided. Consider the next critical thinking activity which deals with this point.

CRITICAL THINKING ACTIVITY 3.4

LEVEL 5

Imagine you are investigating an offence of robbery involving a 15 year-old girl being assaulted in the street and her mobile phone being stolen. A member of the public, Jennifer Starling, who lives on the street, rings the control room a few hours after the incident and states that she saw the robbery. She will not make a witness statement but can identify the offender as Mark Cooke, a 17 year-old who lives a few streets away. The control room operator who takes the call has only worked in a police environment for a few months and copies all of the information and details from the witness, including name and address, into an intelligence report which is entered onto the system without any protective marking.

- What do you think of this example?

- What would your action have been regarding the witness and the information provided?

Sample answers are provided at the end of this book.

GOVERNMENT SECURITY CLASSIFICATION (GSC) OF INFORMATION

This system came into effect in 2014, the objective being to protect all the information generated, collected or used by public bodies including government and law enforcement. It applies to all UK domestic information as well as international interchange, where incoming information will be dealt with using the same protection levels as though it were UK generated (Cabinet Office, 2018). It is a system designed to protect information in accordance with the law (see Chapter 2). This is a relatively simple premise and Table 3.3 briefly explains the three classifications which define the system.

Table 3.3 Government security classifications

Classification	Synopsis
Official	This is the baseline for the system and the default position is that routine information created or processed by the police will not need to be marked 'official'. If something is marked in this way there must be an explanation to accompany the document as to why it is so marked (Cabinet Office, 2018; College of Policing, 2022c).
Secret	This applies to a higher level than routine day-to-day information. Regarding policing, it perhaps applies to organised crime, cases with business or publicity implications or where there is a suspected 'leak' in a particular unit and it would be detrimental to the investigation if the information was not protected.
Top Secret	As you would expect, this is the top tier and would normally be applied to information concerning national threats such as terrorism, cyber-terrorism and cyberspace virus attacks. The nature of national and international security is such that little or no information risk can be permitted (Cabinet Office, 2018).

GOVERNMENT PROTECTIVE MARKING SYSTEM

This is still part of the GSC but allows an increase in protection if information requires it within the Official classification. Because some information may be of a sensitive nature, particularly where harm could result if it were made known or lost, a document can be marked Official-Sensitive, essentially becoming a need-to-know requirement. Documents marked Official-Restricted or Official-Protect are usually a matter of practice or policy within public organisations; both terms apply within the routine Official approach. Some documents or information may be so generic that they do not require a security marking of any type and would be labelled as not protectively marked. Consider the examples in the next critical thinking activity.

CRITICAL THINKING ACTIVITY 3.5

LEVEL 6

1. Information is received from an off-duty police officer that the BMW registered number ABC 123 was parked overnight behind a row of houses in the residential area of the town centre where you work.

2. Imagine you are on duty when you are summoned to the inquiry office of the police station where someone has requested to speak to you. On attending the office you recognise the person to be a woman you arrested several times for shop theft a couple of years previously. You take her to a witness interview room, where she explains that because you always treated her fairly and were never judgemental in dealing with her, she has information for you. Two nights ago she was present at a house in your area when she overheard a conversation between two local Hells Angels members and an Irishman. They were talking about a weapons cache at a private dwelling house about 20 miles away, in particular a high-powered rifle which they intimated had previously been used in two political murders in Europe and had been smuggled into the UK to be used by a Chinese triad. She will only talk to you, she will not repeat the information to anyone else and does not want to be contacted again.

• What do you think the security classification should be in each example?

• What are the reasons for your answer?

Sample answers are provided at the end of this book.

CONCLUSION

Chapter 3 has introduced the concept of intelligence-led policing, explained the central ter-minology used such as strategic and tactical intelligence, and briefly explained the impact of the digital environment and some of the challenges it poses for policing. The NIM has been considered from a practical perspective, alongside relevant examples to assist you in writing an intelligence item and the considerations you should have when doing so. This was accompanied by an explanation of the need to sanitise information and the basic approach for making an assessment of information. Finally, the Government Security Classification scheme and its accompanying protective marking structure were explained, along with how they fit all information within the public sector. If you decide to pursue a career in policing, this chapter equips you with baseline knowledge of intelligence-led policing, the NIM and the basic tools to write and submit intelligence items so that you do not jeopardise yourself, an investigation or the information source.

SUMMARY OF KEY CONCEPTS

This chapter has discussed some of the following key concepts.

⚙ The meaning of the term intelligence-led policing.

⚙ A broad overview of how the digital environment impacts upon investigative information gathering.

⚙ The need for a standardised intelligence model (the NIM) so that the 43 police forces operate in the same way and submit/handle/assess information from the same baseline.

⚙ The purpose of tasking and co-ordinating meetings.

⚙ The stages of GADPO.

⚙ Considerations when grading the information to be submitted using the 3x5 system.

⚙ The reasons for sanitising information.

⚙ How to assess information.

⚙ The Government Security Classification scheme and associated protective marking options for all information within the public sector.

CHECK YOUR KNOWLEDGE

1. What is meant by the term 'intelligence-led' policing?

2. What is the difference between strategic assessment and a tactical assessment of information?

3. What is the objective of the Government Classification System?

4. Why is the provenance, assessment and sanitisation of information important?

5. Explain intelligence assessment ratings A and B.

Sample answers are provided at the end of this book.

FURTHER READING

BOOKS AND BOOK CHAPTERS

Akhgar, B, Bayerl, P S and Sampson, F (eds) (2016) *Open Source Intelligence Investigation*. Cham: Springer International Publishing AG.
This book provides a series of chapters debating the use of open-source internet information, its collection and methods of doing so, tools and concepts as they apply to policing, and handling and obtaining information from the digital environment.

Treverton, G F and Agrell, W (2009) *National Intelligence Systems*. New York: Cambridge University Press.
This is a book which deals with the theoretical concepts of national intelligence issues such as the need for standardisation and T&C systems and the need to improve the understanding of intelligence.

ARTICLES IN JOURNALS

Janjeva, A, Harris, A and Byrne, J (2022) *The Future of Open Source Intelligence for UK National Security*. London: Royal United Services Institute. [online] Available at: https://static.rusi.org/330_OP_FutureOfOpenSourceIntelligence_FinalWeb0.pdf (accessed 3 February 2023).
This occasional paper by the renowned Royal United Services Institute explores the role of social media in a national security context and with a view to informing future public policy on this issue.

John, T and Maguire, M (2004) *The National Intelligence Model: Key Lessons from Early Research.* Home Office. [online] Available at: www.researchgate.net/publication/242484328_The_National_Intelligence_Model_key_lessons_from_early_research (accessed 3 February 2023).
This an online report which, although compiled in 2004, demonstrates the understanding of the NIM shortly after it was initiated and is a useful comparison to the current understanding of policing intelligence.

Kenningdale, P (2020) The National Intelligence Model: The Barriers to Its Success. BSC Policing Network. [online] Available at: https://bscpolicingnetwork.com/2022/05/31/the-national-intelligence-model-the-barriers-to-its-success (accessed 3 February 2023).
This article considers the effectiveness of the NIM and any inhibitors to its better success.

WEBSITES

The College of Policing guidance on intelligence management: www.college.police.uk/app/intelligence-management/intelligence-report

CHAPTER 4
INTELLIGENCE PATHWAYS

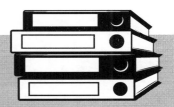

LEARNING OBJECTIVES

AFTER READING THIS CHAPTER YOU WILL BE ABLE TO:

- ⚙ identify the fundamental groupings of intelligence;

- ⚙ understand the links between intelligence and investigations;

- ⚙ distinguish between the different tiers of intelligence pathways;

- ⚙ utilise international links for intelligence gathering;

- ⚙ apply the menu of tactics to enhance intelligence possibilities.

INTRODUCTION

This chapter is not intended to be an in-depth discussion of every intelligence possibility; rather it provides an introductory overview of the central themes to allow you to understand some of the practical complexities within the intelligence context. The aim of this chapter is to identify intelligence pathways for use in all policing inquiries. The current architecture for intelligence progression is explained by utilising six tiers of policing to provide a comprehensive overview of the structure relevant to investigations and other policing inquiries.

Within those tiers are limitless possibilities for accessing information under the legislative parameters explained in Chapter 2. You are then introduced to fundamental groupings of intelligence which you can use to maximise intelligence-gathering opportunities for any investigation and the discussion will focus on how the basic clusters of intelligence possibilities remain fairly constant across the breadth of the law enforcement spectrum. Becoming familiar with those groupings will allow you to begin to recognise where information might be available, how it fits within the existing policing architecture and how to refine your intelligence-gathering possibilities bespoke to your policing inquiry. A menu of tactics assists you in enhancing your intelligence possibilities by thinking more widely, before the chapter concludes by considering international aspects of intelligence co-operation (including the digital environment) and the mechanisms which exist to allow international co-operation.

CRITICAL THINKING ACTIVITY 4.1

LEVEL 4

Imagine it is your first month on duty as a police officer. You have made various inquiries on a criminal case allocated to you to investigate. The case involved a white transit van and after making various diligent inquiries you ascertain information to identify the van and its owner. Resulting from a check via the Police National Computer (PNC), your sergeant approaches you and tells you to halt your investigation and supply all details from your case to the ROCU. No other explanation is offered, and you have no idea what a ROCU is. These circumstances raise two main issues. If you have no context, how will you understand what is being expected of you? How will you present the information and choose an appropriate delivery method?

• Consider what information you would require to fulfil the task you have been given and compare your results to those provided at the end of the book.

Sample answers are provided at the end of this book.

GENERAL INTELLIGENCE AND PRACTICAL POLICING

Before considering the structures within policing which can affect intelligence-handling pathways, we need to briefly consider general intelligence as it applies to a police officer involved in general duties. This is because there is sometimes a perception within policing that the acquisition, analysis and application of intelligence (see Chapter 1) is the role of specially trained intelligence officers. We should begin by dispelling this myth right away. Every police officer has the opportunity during routine duties to acquire information which can rapidly become intelligence and be used to develop intervention points (analysing and developing information to present an available course or courses of action). General policing is the baseline of information gathering as officers go about their daily duties in communities all over the UK. What they observe during the course of those duties is then often used by specialist departments such as CID to solve crime, trace victims and witnesses and recover stolen property.

POLICING SPOTLIGHT

Imagine you work in a city centre. During the course of your duties, particularly early on weekday mornings, you stand for half an hour at the main high street crossroads where you can observe the traffic entering the city and talk to storekeepers as they begin to open up for business (community policing). Over several months you begin to understand the routines that certain people practise every workday as they go about their business. One of the people you observe during this time is a woman in her mid-twenties who only passes by on a Thursday or Friday and always wears a blue and yellow outfit. One night when you are on patrol near the local nightclub a large fight breaks out and you and your colleagues make several arrests for an offence of violent disorder (under the Public Order Act 1986, s.2) *'where three or more people use unlawful violence that could cause a person of reasonable firmness to fear for their safety'*). This is an essential point to prove if you are to obtain a conviction later in court. As you break up the fight you notice a woman walking through the melee who you recognise to be the same woman you have observed some mornings wearing the blue and yellow outfit. By the time the disorder situation has been contained, the woman has gone. CID officers dealing with the incident make it plain they cannot charge any suspects without an independent witness. You remember the woman passing through the fight area and when next on morning shift you wait until she passes by. You approach her and she confirms she did see a large disturbance at the weekend and is prepared to make a witness statement which can be used by CID officers to prosecute all people involved.

This example is based on real-life events and demonstrates how a uniform police officer conducting daily duties is an integral part of the information and intelligence chain. You can never predict which observations or information you accumulate while on the beat may become useful in combatting crime or tracing witnesses, victims or offenders.

THE SIX TIERS OF POLICING

One of the most important factors in intelligence handling is context. Context applies to the information itself, how it was obtained and the architecture (the structure) in which the information is to be applied. It is important to understand that policing within the UK functions widely (43 police forces), and multi-operationally (various specialist regional and national units), as well as on a multi-agency basis (a multitude of agencies including His Majesty's Revenue and Customs, Department for Work and Pensions, over 100 Trading Standards agencies, the Serious Fraud Office, Financial Conduct Authority, and others). Information and intelligence constantly flow through all of these agencies, primarily using the National Intelligence Model (see Chapter 3) at all levels, and it can be confusing to a new officer or policing student as to how it all fits together. Dividing the current UK intelligence into six tiers to indicate where it is used provides the context you require before moving on to consider the groups of intelligence which are available to exploit.

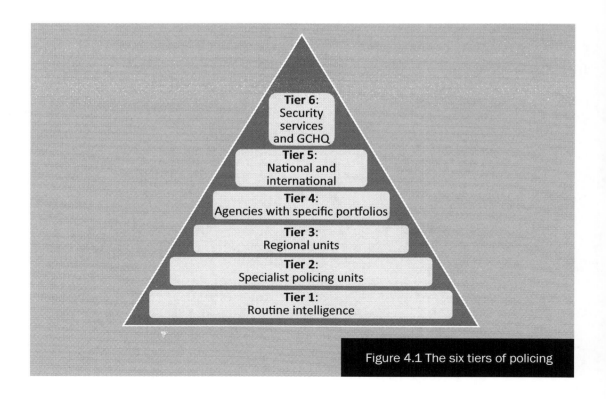

Figure 4.1 The six tiers of policing

TIER 1: ROUTINE INTELLIGENCE AT AN OPERATIONAL POLICING LEVEL

This is the basic tier of intelligence as it applies to routine and everyday duties conducted by uniform constables and detective constables in the community. It includes things like:

- sightings of known criminals by officers while on duty (burglars, shoplifters, car thieves etc) and those individuals who live locally and who are constantly in trouble with the law;

- information from local Neighbourhood Watch groups;

- information from members of the public who have witnessed an incident;

- information about vehicles being used by local criminals (ones to watch out for to stop and check);

- information about events happening within a particular beat area;

- local drug-dealing information;

- anti-social behaviour reports;

- missing person reports;

- local accident blackspots and other risks to public safety;

- local crime prevention initiatives;

- criminal associations;

- where stolen property might be being sold;

- information about nightclubs, licensed premises, late-night refreshment houses;

- information which is not about criminals, but which may impact on policing resources (public events, protest marches, garden fetes, football matches, raves, public gatherings).

You can observe that even from this relatively short list, there is a myriad of information which is useful at a routine policing level. The list is not exhaustive and as per the example in the policing spotlight above, you never know what basic information or observation will be useful.

TIER 2: SPECIALIST POLICING UNITS AND OTHER LAW ENFORCEMENT AGENCIES

This tier includes major crime units, child protection units, volume crime units, robbery squads, cybercrime units, financial investigation units, fraud squads, specialist traffic sections, aerial units and drone operators – essentially any specialist units in policing which are removed from those routine daily duties included in Tier 1. It is within these units that information tends to start to become more refined and targeted at specific streams of criminality or particular incidents. All of these units, and others, are to be found within UK police forces, fulfilling more specialised duties but very much integrating with routine information gathered in Tier 1.

TIER 3: REGIONAL UNITS

In policing terms, this includes the regional organised crime units (ROCUs) and regional asset recovery teams (RARTs). In recent years these units have largely been co-located and have merged to include money laundering, fraud and asset recovery teams, as well as departments dealing with digital crime, intelligence gathering and analysis, Covert Human Intelligence Source handling, threat assessment, undercover and surveillance and other specialist duties. Sometimes there are multi-agency personnel working together within these units (such as His Majesty's Revenue and Customs and Department of Work and Pensions).

Personnel in these units tend to be specialists who deal with cross-border (county to county) criminality which is too complex or simply too resource demanding for one police force to manage but which sits just below the type of criminality which would be undertaken by the National Crime Agency (see Tier 5). Intelligence at this level becomes even more refined, quite often depending on surveillance capabilities, digital interventions and specialist equipment not generally available in many police forces primarily due to cost. These units still depend on Tier 1 information being fed into the NIM. Check out the following policing spotlight to see the effect of routine information and a specialist unit outcome.

CRITICAL THINKING ACTIVITY 4.2

LEVEL 5

Information is received that a drugs shipment is being collected in a specific motor car for which you are also provided with the make, model and registration plate. The vehicle will be driven by 'Jim', a local small-time drug dealer on behalf of a collection of other drug dealers. Jim is to take £25,000 south using the M6 motorway and deliver it to a person in a white Range Rover motor car which will be parked at a motorway services past junction 12.

Either an exchange of the money for drugs will take place at the services or the recipient vehicle will accept the cash and leave and subsequently return with the drugs being purchased.

- What would your recommended action be if this information were received? While considering what action you would take, assume that the information is from a covert human intelligence source and has been deemed as accurate as it can be.

Sample answers are provided at the end of this book.

TIER 4: AGENCIES WITH SPECIFIC PORTFOLIOS BEYOND GENERAL POLICING

Examples of these types of agency are the Serious Fraud Office, Marine Management Organisation, The Insolvency Service, His Majesty's Revenue and Customs, and the Financial Conduct Authority. Once again, the list is not exhaustive and each one of these agencies has a particular remit to fulfil. The implication for intelligence flow is that the legal parameters explained in Chapter 2 may affect the way in which information is passed between such agencies, either between themselves or between them and the police. Very often, information flow becomes part of a working agreement between agencies. These are usually in two forms.

1. A service-level agreement (SLA), which is usually a long-standing document and usually formulated to cope with constant demands in one area of information flow. A good example would be police officers who need to identify the National Insurance number of a suspect. The standing agreement between the Department for Work and Pensions and all police forces is that this can be achieved via a set framework to control the information flow but not at the detriment to practical efficiency in obtaining a result.

2. A memorandum of understanding (MOU) is a document between one or two agencies who will be working together for a short period of time or on one specific investigation. It allows those agencies to exchange information within the restrictions of GDPR and other relevant legislation for only that period of time. Once the joint working ends, so does the MOU (see Chapter 6).

All of the agencies falling into this category may work on national or international investigations which generally are outside general policing responsibilities.

TIER 5: NATIONAL AND INTERNATIONAL CRIMINALITY

These areas are dealt with primarily by the National Crime Agency (NCA), who lead the UK's fight to cut serious and organised crime, protecting the public by targeting and pursuing those criminals who pose the greatest risk to the UK.

All of the previous tiers feed into the NCA where necessary and legislation allows information to be shared with the NCA without infringing on existing data protection legislation. The activities of the NCA may integrate at various times with all other tiers depending on the locality and breadth of any investigation undertaken. In the Crime and Courts Act 2013, two central statutory functions are created for the NCA:

- crime reduction;

- a criminal intelligence function.

The NCA's first priority is to identify and disrupt serious organised crime and to prioritise cybercrime, economic crime, child sexual exploitation and human trafficking (National Crime Agency, 2015).

In the case of terrorism or any international criminality such as arms dealing which may pose a threat to the national security of the UK, the NCA is likely to exchange intelligence with the national security services explained in Tier 6.

TIER 6: SECURITY SERVICES AND THE GOVERNMENT COMMUNICATIONS HEADQUARTERS (GCHQ)

You may have wondered at some point what the acronyms MI5 and MI6 actually stand for. The answer is military intelligence; MI5 has the national intelligence brief and MI6 the international brief. These are supplemented by GCHQ, which the public generally perceive as the UK 'listening post'. The task of GCHQ is to collect communications and other data, analyse that data and produce real-world outcomes to counter terrorist or cyber threats against the UK (GCHQ, 2022). As a serving police officer engaged in general duties, you may think that these agencies are too remote to have any contact with. There is often more contact than you would think. At any major incident, these specialist units will depend on local intelligence such as local community, cultural and geographical knowledge.

POLICING SPOTLIGHT

Imagine you are on duty when information is received that somewhere in the Middle East, a body has been found after a failed terrorist bombing attack abroad. The body has been identified by the security services as being from the area you routinely police as a uniform or detective constable. At a briefing when you are next on duty, you are asked to provide any information about the identity of the body which has been found and for information about family or community connections. When the name of the individual is identified at the briefing you realise that you know the family, who live within the neighbourhood area you routinely patrol. The inquiry team is desperate for information and suddenly you are the one who can provide it in terms of background to the family and the area.

The six tiers are designed to make it easier to understand how intelligence flows between layers of policing and where information pathways already exist or can be forged. Any piece of information can become important at any level, and that information or intelligence can flow up or down the tiers. This structure, specially created for this book, enables you to understand that as a police officer (or any other law enforcement officer) you may be called into an investigation at any time because of basic knowledge you possess and no one else does.

INTELLIGENCE GROUPINGS

Information can come from any source and eventually become active intelligence. It can then be used to create intervention points such as tracing individuals, identifying stolen goods, stop and search events, traffic roadblocks – the list is endless. The number of sources from which information can be gathered is impossible to list. It is, however, possible to create general intelligence groupings to help to provide context for the myriad of different sources.

Table 4.1 summarises these groupings and can be applied to intelligence gathering in all proactive and reactive investigations, regardless of whether they are criminal or civil in nature. Before you conduct any checks, it is always a good idea to think about what criminality you are pursuing or trying to detect. Remember that criminals do not always stick to one type of crime. It is important to remember that the grouping column simply states the general heading within which there is usually an endless array of checks you can conduct. Some of these are included to give you an idea of what sits within each one.

Table 4.1 Grouping information sources

Grouping	Description
Standard initial police checks	Police National Computer (PNC) checks – name, address, date of birth, passport checks, address checks, previous convictions.
Other law enforcement agencies	Surrounding local police forces, National Crime Agency, Trading Standards.
Government agencies	His Majesty's Revenue and Customs (HMRC), Department for Work and Pensions (DWP), Marine Management Organisation, Gangmasters and Labour Abuse Authority, local council.
Associated criminality	Look wider than the offence you are initially considering. A drug dealer can still be a human trafficker.
Victims, witnesses and scene of the incident	What does the scene of a crime tell you? What information is available from any witnesses or victim(s)?
Home address	Identify premises and who owns it (or them).
Familial links	Basic family tree and associated addresses.
Associates	Friends (including any with previous convictions), business partners, previous prison cellmates.
Communications	Landline, email, mobile phones.
Vehicles	Owner, leased, pool car (used by a pool of criminals to complicate audit trail as to who owns the vehicle).
Business	Any connected business links/individuals/vehicles/shop premises/storage capabilities locally, regionally and internationally.
Travel	Local/regional/national/international. Destination? Who with? Cost? Frequency?
Financial	Lifestyle (gym memberships, clubs, gambling habits), premises, assets, investments, bank accounts, credit cards.
Digital information (known as the digital footprint)	Digital links such as Facebook, Instagram, Twitter etc, eBay, LinkedIn, business website(s). Don't forget Google and media outlets.
Technical deployment	Surveillance, listening posts, tracker devices.

These groupings serve as a checklist of intelligence areas which do not change over time. The groupings inform us of what may be available and where to begin looking. Once located, the law determines parameters for lawfully obtaining information (see Chapter 2). The information possibilities within each grouping are unlimited.

The newest addition is of course the digital footprint and with the constant expansion of the internet, new criminal activities also offer new possibilities for intelligence. Those possibilities are all within the grouping of digital intelligence. Therefore, when you find yourself approaching an investigation or other inquiry, you already have a list of key areas to consider before you drill down into the myriad of possibilities each grouping offers. This integrates well with the principle of investigative strategy, the planning tool used to control the avenues of inquiry and resources.

REFLECTIVE PRACTICE 4.1

LEVEL 4

When tasked with any inquiry or investigation, the groupings are there to remind you of the possibilities available. You may find yourself routinely using tools such as the PNC, previous conviction checks and address checks so often that it becomes second nature. Where you use something new in a particular grouping it would be good practice to make a list to remind you of where you have been or who you approached for information. Investigations differ significantly and if you are conducting multiple inquiries, it is easy to forget information or lose contacts or the details of the solution you discovered. A working document listing contact details is easily designed and maintained.

- Formulate a table or use a spreadsheet. The key to success is to keep your list updated (whatever form you choose). Table 4.2 provides a rudimentary example. Obviously, you can include whatever details you want, and your table or spreadsheet can be as comprehensive as you want to make it.

Table 4.2 Contact details tracker

Date	Organisation	Contact	Contact details	Product
16/03/22	Force HQ	Jenny Wren	45678 12345	Crime pattern analyst
26/01/22	NCA	Joe Smith	01234 123456	Intelligence charting
14/03/22	Serious Fraud Office	Ella Fitz	12345 23456	Expert in offshore trusts

If you move from one policing unit to another you will take your contact list with you, and it will grow throughout your service and always be up to date. Not all tools and options are used in every inquiry. A working and updateable list will ensure the widest information opportunities within each grouping, no matter what your investigation might be. The example in Table 4.2 is ordered alphabetically by organisation so information can be more easily retrieved (see Chapter 6 for further information).

CRITICAL THINKING ACTIVITY 4.3

LEVEL 6

You are tasked with investigating a man known to work as a doorman at a local nightclub who is suspected to be dealing cannabis as people enter and leave. You are supplied with his name and address.

- Identify the groupings which would offer possibilities you could use to gather information to verify or disprove the intelligence you have received.

- After you have exhausted any routine checks, what other action could you take to support any police-held information you have found?

Sample answers are provided at the end of this book.

LINKING INTELLIGENCE TO INVESTIGATIONS

For most routine investigations, current thinking is that an intelligence strategy is not required (College of Policing, 2013). Cases are small and usually dealt with quickly on a day-to-day basis.

In larger and more complex investigations it is essential to use an investigative strategy. This is simply a record of what is being investigated and why, the routes of investigation being pursued and the resources available or deployed. Any information or intelligence requirements can be included in the strategy document in order to keep track of opportunities, possibilities and any intervention outcomes which result. This approach also fits well with the legal obligations concerning intelligence gathering (see Chapter 2), in particular the rationale for decisions made and human rights aspects.

When an operation results in an arrest, searches and a successful prosecution, it is tempting to think that the case is closed but this is not necessarily the case. Cases have a way of opening themselves up again and the best tool in your investigation armoury is an open mind. When you think that you have all the facts and the conclusion has been reached, a thorough debrief may save issues emerging later. Consider the following reflective practice example.

REFLECTIVE PRACTICE 4.2

LEVEL 5

Information from a Covert Human Intelligence Source (CHIS) is received regarding 20 kilos of cannabis resin being transferred from the north to the south of England for onward sale. Specific information is received and an intelligence package is created, which leads to the transit van being stopped and two men arrested on suspicion of trafficking drugs. The van is searched and 10 kilos of cannabis are located in the side and floor panels of the van, indicated by a search-trained drugs dog. As the transit van is a rental van, and after forensic tests have been conducted for additional evidence, it is returned to the hire company. Everyone is happy with the outcome and the information regarding 20 kilos was thought to be wrong and in fact it was always a 10-kilo load. Approximately 18 months later, after prosecution and conviction, a former CHIS who had been prosecuted and convicted for other non-connected offences called officers to the prison they were in. The CHIS was adamant that the load in the van was 20 kilos and would not be moved. Officers returned to their unit and submitted the information to the NIM.

- What do you think happened with the information and why?

Sample answers are provided at the end of this book.

CONTEXT

The key word for linking information to investigations is *context*. Without context, information is generally useless.

The link between information and an investigation may be a straightforward connection such as a witness to a road accident informing you of the registration number of the car responsible, which has driven off from the scene without the driver leaving their details. You will still need to check the information and corroborate it where you can, but this is a simple situation where information is immediately linked to an event.

It becomes more complicated when you may already have information but without context, as in the policing spotlight below.

POLICING SPOTLIGHT

A local and well-known drug dealer (Brown) is stopped by patrol officers and while issuing a form for the driver to produce his insurance details, one of the officers takes note of a post office box number (53) lying on the front car seat. On returning to the police station, the officers input details of the stop/check and the post office box number into the intelligence system. When the regional organised crime unit check the system while conducting an investigation into Brown (unbeknown to local officers) they note the vehicle stop but, more importantly, the post office box number. When this is checked it identifies a different individual (with an address) who has paid for the box number in order to have mail delivered to it. When the address is checked, it turns out to be in the name of the suspect's grandfather but paid for by an offshore company. This eventually leads to offshore bank accounts being identified for the suspect, who, when arrested some months later, finds out that his overseas assets have all been frozen, subject to the case outcome.

This real-life spotlight shows that at Tier 1 level the information is gathered by one set of officers who have no context for what they have found. They did their job by reporting the details of the post office box without alerting the suspect, even though they had no knowledge of whether the information was useful or not. At another level, the information regarding the post office box became intelligence with an actionable outcome and which provided evidence to be used on arrest. Once again, a specialist unit relied on information gathered from routine policing (Tier 1 to Tier 3).

MENU OF TACTICS

Primarily developed as a directory of alternative methods to generate information about and to investigate serious and organised criminality, the menu of tactics is something that all routine investigators should be aware of. Many of the information pathways within it can be useful for routine investigations as well as those which are more complex and usually the remit of specialist units.

It certainly integrates with the principle of intelligence-led policing (see Chapter 3), as well as underpinning the current governmental CONTEST strategy for countering terrorist activity of Pursue, Prevent, Protect and Prepare (the four Ps), which is in place to deter serious and organised crime as well as terrorist activity (HM Government, 2018).

EVIDENCE-BASED POLICING

Alexandra Cook is suspected of supplying class A and class B drugs and had invested money into the purchase of a piece of land ten years prior to the current criminal investigation starting. A total of 37 different companies have been used to conceal ownership of the land and over 40 storage units which had been built on it. It is suspected that some of the storage units are being used to facilitate the storage of drugs but the information is circumstantial. Cook has proven difficult to investigate because she only uses family members to conduct her criminal activities and it has been impossible to use either a CHIS or an undercover officer to obtain information. A site survey by one of the static observation teams in the early stages of the investigation included photographs of the land and the premises on it. On seeing the photographs, an officer who had previously worked with the local council noticed four large billboards had been erected at one end of the land. They appear to be currently used for advertising beauty products. Checks with the advertiser revealed that £900 per month is paid for the board space. The officer suggests checking with the council to see if planning permission is required for large advertising billboards and, if so, whether any was applied for by the owner of the property. The planning officer confirmed that planning permission is required for such boards and that, in this case, no application had been made. Letters were sent to the various businesses registered against the land, threatening to remove the billboards. This eventually forced Cook to come forward and defend herself against the planning permission being revoked. Once Cook's identity as the owner of the land had been established, the audit trail to company ownership became clear, as did the ownership of another two million pounds' worth of assets. The owner was arrested and prosecuted for money laundering and a total of £34,000 in cash was seized. The alternative method using planning permission infractions enabled the main prosecution case to be made.

The central idea of the menu of tactics is to disrupt criminal activity using alternative means if traditional investigative methods prove inefficient or ineffective. It can be used by any law enforcement agency and extensively covers a range of options under the headings of business, crime, travel, vehicle, behaviour and lifestyle (College of Policing, 2022d). Over 70 different agencies and businesses contribute to the menu of tactics and it will continue to develop under the guidance of the NCA.

INTERNATIONAL ASPECTS OF INTELLIGENCE

The first thing to note here is that arrangements for the interchange of intelligence since the UK left the European Union have changed. To support these changes, in 2018, the International Crime Coordination Centre (ICCC) was established to advise on issues such as extradition, judicial co-operation, criminal and terrorist watchlists and general police co-operation. A knowledge hub has been created that you can join as a police officer, and which encourages collaboration to share information between police forces and the private sector (College of Policing, 2023).

Most police forces now have at least one international liaison officer who acts as a single point of contact for inquiries in the force and from abroad. This role integrates with each region in the UK having two similar liaison posts as part of the ICCC and whose support role includes three areas:

1. routine policing – inquiries concerning foreign nationals who are in the UK;

2. transnational investigations – exchanging information and evidence internationally;

3. illegal entry to the UK of foreign nationals (people smuggling or asylum seekers) (College of Policing, 2022e).

An essential point to note here is never to directly contact a foreign police force or any other institution without first ascertaining your force protocols for doing so. You do not want to be the cause of an international argument over jurisdiction.

Even though the UK has left the European Union, as part of the withdrawal agreement separate steps were taken to recognise the UK as a third-party state, which means that UK policing can still engage with Europol and the Eurojust website that supports joint investigation teams (Eurojust, 2022). Other facilities also continue to exist which, for example, allow DNA profiles and fingerprints to be checked bilaterally (available for missing persons as well as criminals, witnesses and victims). Unfortunately, leaving the EU has resulted in the UK being withdrawn from the Schengen Agreement, which provided intelligence alerts regarding people and property.

MUTUAL LEGAL ASSISTANCE

Overseas inquiries usually require a formal application to be made, usually by the Crown Prosecution Service. These are currently referred to as ILORs (international letters of request) and are created where specific evidence has been identified and is required to support the prosecution of an offender (see Chapter 6).

THE INTERNET

Throughout the previous chapters it has become apparent that the internet has altered not only the way criminals have adapted their activity to make use of it, but also the way in which UK policing has had to adapt its investigative and intelligence methods. The latest crime figures from the Office for National Statistics show that crime has undergone an extensive migration into the digital environment (the internet), exacerbated by the Covid-19 pandemic. Since October 2021, there has been a 37 per cent increase in fraud and computer misuse offences. This translates into 4.535 million offences of fraud and a further 1.633 million computer misuse offences (ONS, 2022). Many of these offences will have an international link. The problem is that the same protocols for identifying and gathering evidence exist for internet information as they do for real-world crime. This means that although criminals have no restrictions and can commit offences in multiple international jurisdictions in a single day, law enforcement can only move slowly while adhering to international agreements, protocols and legislation. Mutual legal assistance is still required (see Chapter 6).

CRITICAL THINKING ACTIVITY 4.4

LEVEL 5

Imagine you are investigating a series of high-value dwelling house burglaries and arrest John Smith, a local antiques dealer suspected of handling or money laundering the property. You have information from his computer which suggests that Smith has purchased land in Thailand and you establish he is married to a Thai wife. The forensic examination of a laptop seized during the search of Smith's shop suggests the land or property in Thailand may have been bought involving cryptocurrency (digital money).

• What do you think your options are in the circumstances described?

Sample answers are provided at the end of this book.

CONCLUSION

This chapter has introduced you to the six tiers which form law enforcement architecture within the UK and thereby offer context for any police information and the pathway it might take. You have also been familiarised with intelligence groupings which, as broad headings, do not change. Within them is a myriad of information possibilities.

In turn, this, and the context in which intelligence is given, contributes to the potential offered by the menu of tactics and thinking laterally when gathering intelligence. By all means, pursue the traditional routes which you are likely to have been taught or at least introduced to but then consider other alternatives which can produce great results. Choose one which will catch most criminals by surprise. Information management has been discussed in terms of intelligence, before ending the chapter by considering the impact of the digital environment and the current pathways available to obtain information from other jurisdictions. The practical examples accompanying all of this discussion demonstrate the practical translation of this knowledge into practical policing within an intelligence context.

SUMMARY OF KEY CONCEPTS

This chapter has discussed some of the following key concepts.

- Different tiers of policing and how they integrate with one another.

- Using the NIM to submit information on a routine basis even if it seems far-fetched (such as in Critical thinking activity 4.2 regarding the buried cash).

- Groupings of intelligence repositories do not really change and within these groupings are a myriad of avenues you can pursue for information.

- There is no information that is unworthy of attention.

- How to design a living document spreadsheet which manages your contacts as your policing career progresses and which you can easily keep up to date electronically.

- The advantages of thinking more widely and utilising opportunities such as those mentioned in the menu of tactics.

- Crime is migrating into the digital environment (obtaining intelligence from the internet can be achieved locally but if a foreign jurisdiction is involved, any formal evidence at their end must be obtained by way of an ILOR as defined in international agreements).

CHECK YOUR KNOWLEDGE

1. How many tiers of policing are there?

2. Name five of the intelligence groupings.

3. Why is information relatively useless without context?

4. What is the International Crime Coordination Centre?

5. When is an ILOR required?

Sample answers are provided at the end of this book.

FURTHER READING

BOOKS AND BOOK CHAPTERS

Ratcliffe, J (2016) *Intelligence-led Policing.* Oxon: Routledge.
This book explains the origins of intelligence-led policing and its impact upon crime, and questions whether it prevents crime. Case studies are used to underpin the arguments made.

ARTICLES IN JOURNALS

HM Government (2011) *Prevent Strategy.* [online] Available at: https://assets.publishing. service.gov.uk/government/uploads/system/uploads/attachment_data/file/97976/ prevent-strategy-review.pdf (accessed 3 February 2022).
This government review will help you think about the origin of the Prevent strategy and the rationale in today's policing environment.

WEBSITES

Gov.UK: www.gov.uk/government/publications/counter-terrorism-strategy-contest-2018 (accessed 31 August 2022).
This website has the latest CONTEST strategy and information on Pursue, Prevent, Protect and Prepare.

CHAPTER 5
INTELLIGENCE ANALYSIS

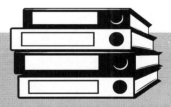

LEARNING OBJECTIVES

AFTER READING THIS CHAPTER YOU WILL BE ABLE TO:

- ⚙ understand how the intelligence cycle works and why it is an important process;

- ⚙ apply methods of sanitisation to intelligence items;

- ⚙ evaluate information;

- ⚙ identify bias and its effect on intelligence outcomes;

- ⚙ apply a critical mindset to the evaluation of information to produce intelligence outcomes;

- ⚙ analyse information based upon its own merit and remove any automatic process which may lead to assumptions being made.

INTRODUCTION

Once information has been gathered in either small or large quantities, a process is required to assess that information to identify potential outcomes (where action can be taken) or to identify further avenues of information gathering.

This chapter discusses the intelligence cycle, how intelligence is evaluated and how an intelligence assessment is made. Consideration is given to the evaluation of information and quality assurance issues, including any risk assessments required. The origins of information and any potential bias posed by its source is discussed, together with any requirements for intelligence dissemination such as any sanitisation required (this links with the initial information provided in Chapter 1 concerning what to do in terms of a court trial and public interest immunity).

EVIDENCE-BASED POLICING

The police are notified via the relevant prison liaison officer that Simon Smith, a convicted drug dealer, is due to leave prison in two days' time after serving eight years' imprisonment. On the same day, information is received from a Covert Human Intelligence Source (CHIS) that Simon has asked some of his associates to dig up a quantity of cash which he had buried before he went to prison, ready for his release. Then he would be 'off to Spain'. When additional questions are asked of the CHIS, it is established that the information was overheard by the CHIS while in a room with Simon's ex-wife at a family party. The ex-wife had overheard a close associate of Simon who was drunk, and she remembered him saying that Simon would be okay when he was released from prison because he had cash reserves buried at his old property. No value was mentioned, and neither was an address.

The information from the CHIS was passed to a serious and organised crime unit, where opinion was divided about the information. Most of the experienced detectives in the room were convinced that the information was the general ramblings of a drunken man who wanted to be the centre of attention; they dismissed it out of hand. The information was also two years old and they had received many so-called intelligence items in the past which never provided any result.

One of the detectives liaised with an attached intelligence cell and persuaded them to check out where the 'old property' might be and it was established that Simon had lived at a property in Lancashire which backed onto open fields.

After significant debate, the detective managed to persuade a senior officer that observations at the rear of the property in Lancashire should continue, notwithstanding how old the information appeared to be. Because the 'old property' could be identified, this lent some credence to the possibility that the information, coinciding with Simon's release, might have some substance.

Observations continued and on the second day (the day before Simon's release) a flatback lorry appeared outside the property. Three men got out of the vehicle and started to erect a fence where the garden bordered the adjacent field. When they had dug their third post-hole, one of them was seen to retrieve a bag-shaped object from the hole. The three men immediately stopped work, got in the van and left. They were stopped a short distance away and the bag was found to contain over £800,000 in cash.

- What points do you think this evidence-based example demonstrates?

Sample answers are provided at the end of this book.

This chapter is not intended to be an in-depth discussion of all available analysis techniques; it is an introductory-level overview of intelligence analysis as it applies to routine policing. The impact of intelligence dissemination is discussed and how community tension indicators may have a bearing upon the application of the intelligence from a practical perspective (race relations, religious considerations etc). The chapter discusses how to write an intelligence item and the importance of sanitisation of information in certain circumstances. Problem-oriented policing will be examined using the SARA model of information assessment (Scanning, Analysis, Response and Assessment), a process which does not necessarily sit with the National Intelligence Model (NIM), and which applies outside of the sphere of criminal intelligence analysis. The discussion would not be complete without reference to the critical mindset required when dealing with intelligence and the requirement for objectivity by removing any automatic process from the analysis of information.

THE INTELLIGENCE CYCLE

This is a widely accepted (although sometimes contested) conceptual framework, often used to facilitate a basic understanding of the component parts of the process through which information can flow on its journey to become what we would generally refer to as 'intelligence' (Richards, 2010). The idea of the cycle is that each piece of information can be put through a process which tests it and disseminates the result in a consistent way to inform decision making about investigations, incidents or policy making at any level. If you check out any law enforcement information about intelligence, how it is gathered and how it is used, you will usually find a variation of the intelligence cycle. The odd thing is that despite its continued popularity as a concept in law enforcement, academic and government policy, its specific origin appears to have been lost to time. It is generally accepted that it was historically developed for military intelligence requirements but has since been popularised by policing.

Have a look at Figure 5.1.

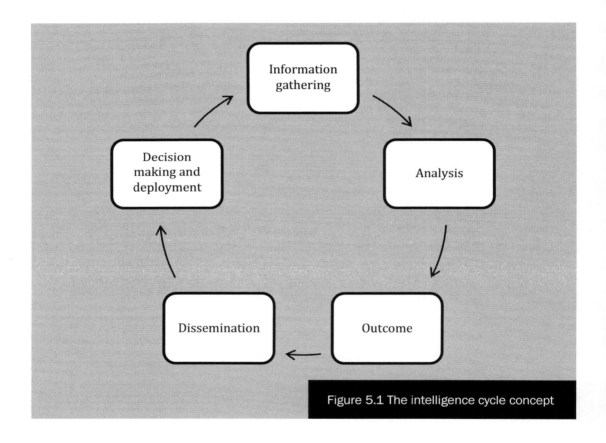

Figure 5.1 The intelligence cycle concept

The idea is that every piece of information is put through the cycle for it to be processed into intelligence. Intelligence can then be used in many ways. As identified by Ribaux et al (2003), the intelligence cycle is the mechanism which produces avenues of investigation that can be pursued and incorporated into operational aspects. Any further information obtained simply triggers another round of the cycle, and so on.

THE INTELLIGENCE CYCLE CONCEPT EXPLAINED

Table 5.1 The intelligence cycle explained

Aspect	Explanation
Information	The starting point of the cycle is that information is received, supplied or discovered.
Analysis	The information is considered in some way so that it can be tested, its origin accounted for, and its accuracy or its relation to other pieces of information already held verified.
Outcome	Can the information be used after it has been processed, considered or analysed? Has the information been verified as usable intelligence and what does the product look like?
Dissemination	What should be done with the intelligence? Where should it now go in order to be effectively used or applied?
Decision	Does the intelligence offer any intervention point? In other words, does it suggest any potential course of action or a potential result if it is used?
Application	This step is something I feel is missed on occasion, and it is also linked to the need for a debriefing if intelligence is used (to consider how the intelligence was applied, what any outcome was and whether it could have been more effective in any way).

There are, of course, times when the practical needs of policing mean that information must be acted on straight away without the luxury of formally utilising the intelligence cycle. Information would still be checked and the provenance established in all circumstances to make sure the intended action to be taken has been tested in some fashion. This may occur as a live situation continues to develop and may be conducted by personnel on the ground.

What this really means is that any information is considered as objectively as possible (depending on the immediacy or time constraints due to any live response required). It may be a situation where information analysis is required immediately (such as a firearms situation) and there is no time to put the information into the NIM and a formal analysis procedure.

This means there are two ways for information analysis to be conducted.

1. Real-time analysis in live situations, usually conducted by police officers at routine and tactical levels (as situations develop, they require an immediate response).

2. Slow-time response which allows the opportunity to further test and establish the provenance of information, analyse it in more detail and effectively plan intervention activities (stop checks, arrests, searches etc).

Consider the following activity and how information might be gathered and processed as part of a real-time scenario at a routine policing level.

CRITICAL THINKING ACTIVITY 5.1

LEVEL 5

Imagine you are on uniform night patrol duty at 0130 hours. You are walking down a residential housing street when you see two men come out from one of the buildings. They are both carrying an assortment of items and as you start to approach them, one sees you and they both drop the items and run off. You run after them and pass over the items noticing they are electrical and at least one of them is a games console. As you pass the front door of the house you see the glass is smashed. A short chase continues and as the two men split up you call for back-up and keep chasing one of the men. You are about 100 metres away and see the man enter a block of flats. Other units have arrived, and you gain access to the main corridor of the flats. An elderly resident approaches you, disturbed by the noise, and she tells you that a man out of breath has gone into flat number 4. You discuss your powers with your colleagues as each flat is not a public space. You ask the lady to describe the person she saw, and the description matches the clothing of the man you chased. Two of your colleagues go around to the rear of the premises while you and another colleague knock on the door of Flat 4. A young woman answers the door but denies anyone has entered since she went to bed some hours ago. You consider all the events and information to date and make a decision.

- Can you identify the intelligence cycle at work in these events? Expand on your answer.

- Identify and explain the process you used to make your decision.

Sample answers are provided at the end of this book.

It is important when you have gathered information that you examine it thoroughly and analyse it for any options it offers you. If you are lucky enough to have access to an analyst, this may be done for you but, even so, it is wise to check that all options have been covered. If you are the one analysing information, it is important to keep an open mind and think beyond the offence that is central to the investigation. If your scope of thinking is narrow, you are likely to miss something. Context for the information you have gathered and a good working knowledge of the law will assist in your examination of the information and the potential for intervention points arising from it.

Consider the following policing spotlight which deals with this point.

POLICING SPOTLIGHT

OLD INFORMATION AND A NEW PAIR OF EYES

Imagine you are asked to assist a specialist unit with an investigation as more staff are required. The major crime unit have been investigating a woman, Edith Jones, who is suspected of drug trafficking for about four months. Since the inception of the investigation over 2000 separate pieces of information have been entered into the intelligence system. Mobile surveillance has been tried over six weeks but without any success other than establishing she never travels anywhere at speed (making it difficult to follow her). Static observations revealed nothing suspicious at the home address. An associated business was uncovered, which consisted of three separate gymnasiums in the local area. Inquiries and static observations on each of these only revealed that several people using them were known criminals and associates of Jones. Both she and her husband had been identified at all three properties. After a few days of trawling through the various surveillance logs, you ask if either Jones or her husband has an online presence. You are told they both have email addresses, which have been identified, as well as an eBay account in the husband's name which is linked to the gymnasiums.

Very quickly you establish that the husband is selling pills online as a gym supplement, even posing for the labels himself. This information has been on file for two weeks after the start date of the investigation. You quickly establish that the payments made for the pills via a linked PayPal account are transferred straight into his wife's account. The question remains as to what the pills actually are. A test purchase is arranged, and the pills are analysed.

The results are sent to the Medicines and Healthcare Products Regulatory Agency, who confirm that the pills are a class C drug and therefore require a licence to be sold. Neither Jones nor her husband is registered to make and trade the pills. Class C medicines offer an arrest power under the Misuse of Drugs Act 1971, and all of the money they have made from non-licensed illegal sale of the pills (estimated from known eBay sales to be a minimum of £125,000) is criminal property. This means that Jones and her husband can be arrested on suspicion of drug trafficking a class C medicine and for money laundering connected to the money made.

- What do you think is the underlying point being made here in terms of intelligence analysis?

Sample answers are provided at the end of this book.

ASSESSMENT OF INTELLIGENCE

This is usually divided into two areas: strategic intelligence assessment and tactical intelligence assessment.

Strategic assessment is designed and intended to provide an overview of any longer-term issues with potential to affect a police force or part of it. Very often it will include strategic partners such as councils or other agencies where they are appropriate to any decision-making concerning emerging trends or public perceptions (College of Policing, 2022b).

Tactical assessment deals with the more short-term issues, identifying subjects, intervention points and any additional needs before recommending the available tactical options which could be applied. This fits well with the NIM as part of the tasking and co-ordination aspect of its structure and is utilised daily by police forces.

Either way, and whether an analyst is used or not, a routine practical guide for officers having to deal with information and any outcomes (action to be taken) is as follows.

- Identify and check the source of the information.

- Understand the context of the information.

- Identify the offence(s) under investigation.

- Identify the objective(s) of the investigation.

- Gather information in line with and in support of the objective(s) of the investigation.

- Test information as it is gathered.

- Only gather relevant material as far as possible. (There is a danger of gathering too much information just because you are able to do so.)

- Take action as rapidly as possible. Old intelligence is unreliable so do not let information become stale.

WRITING AN INTELLIGENCE REPORT FOR EVALUATION

This can be tricky and is not as straightforward as simply writing down everything you know. Information should always be written and submitted in a sanitised way to protect informants, systems and methods of investigation and to mitigate any risk to individuals involved. In serious or terrorist cases, this could include risk to police officers as well as members of the public if certain details were included in the intelligence item without careful thought.

Intelligence can be received anonymously of course, but a large amount of information is submitted by members of the public who provide their details when contacting the police, but who do not want to become involved in any other way such as providing a witness statement. Very often individuals will ring the police with information but do not want to get involved, presenting a problem regarding how the information is not only passed on but also gathered in the first place. For example, if a member of the public reports drug dealing involving youths in a cul-de-sac street and the information is not sanitised as it is being submitted into the NIM, it may be easy to work out where the informant lives. With this point clear in your mind, consider the following example.

REFLECTIVE PRACTICE 5.1

LEVEL 5

Imagine an officer attends a local nightclub where there has been a report of a serious assault. The officer quickly learns that it is a party evening for some local businesses, but an argument escalated and a man was badly injured. A female witness has provided her details and explains what has happened. She asks that neither her name nor details be released at any point because her boss (who has fled the scene) is the person who committed the assault. She refuses to make a witness statement but does provide clear details of what happened. By the time the officer returns to the police station it is almost time to go off duty, but they know that the morning shift will want information, as CID will deal with the case. The officer quickly submits their information as follows.

'Scene of an assault at Flamingo Park nightclub attended as result of radio call. A man had been badly assaulted with injuries to ribs and face, with a suspected broken arm as well. Sheila Stanford, a witness at the scene, explained that her boss Albert Smythe had taken exception about a joke concerning his daughter. Known to have a quick temper, Smythe picked up an unopened wine bottle and began to beat the victim. Stanford will not make a statement because she is scared that if she gets involved, she will get the sack. Stanford sounds like a right piece of work and I wouldn't want to work for him.'

- What are your thoughts about this scenario and the intelligence submission the officer made?

Sample answers are provided at the end of this book.

EVALUATION OF INTELLIGENCE

This is a process which must be conducted objectively if intelligence is to be used effectively. The consistent problem is human nature and the way in which the human mind operates. There is a multitude of biases that are pitfalls when analysing information, which have been discussed at length by academics and psychologists (Ciampaglia and Menczer, 2018; Ling, 2020). These include:

- cognitive bias (flawed patterns of thinking);

- confirmation bias (interpreting new information to confirm your pre-existing belief);

- self-serving bias (take the glory, blame when ineffectual);

- inattentional blindness (missing the point directly before you because your mind is focused somewhere else) (Simple Psychology, 2022).

There are many others and tomes of literature are available on this subject. For the purposes of this chapter, it is clearer to focus on what *not* to do when evaluating information. There are certain things which you must avoid when conducting an evaluation.

Here are Ten Commandments created to assist you when conducting any evaluation of information to provide actionable intelligence.

THE TEN COMMANDMENTS OF INFORMATION EVALUATION

1. Identify the problem you are trying to solve or the objective you are attempting to attain.

2. Do not assume anything. Let the information speak for itself.

3. Do not approach any information with a pre-conceived notion of what it will tell you.

4. Do not jump to conclusions based on the first piece(s) of information you consider.

5. Do not pick and choose which pieces of intelligence you see as favourable to your investigation and ignore the rest.

6. Do not conceal or avoid information simply because it does not fit your idea of what appears to be happening in an investigation.

7. Do not rely on personal or group biases and ignore outside influences such as media.

8. Do not make information 'fit' a set of circumstances. It will either confirm or deny your position without your assistance in bending it to your will.

9. Do not dismiss information because it contradicts your current position.

10. Develop and prepare recommendations from your evaluation of all of the information, no matter whether aligned with or contradictory to the investigation. Present your evaluation in the 'round'.

REFLECTIVE PRACTICE 5.2

LEVEL 5

Imagine you are on uniform patrol when a message comes across the radio. A man has just been chased from a major clothing store after attempting to steal clothing and when challenged by a store detective he assaulted them, causing a head injury. The man is described as being two metres tall, well built and wearing a dark blue puffer jacket and dark trousers. Approximately ten minutes later, you see a man of similar description, except he is wearing light-coloured trousers, walking towards you and away from the area where the incident occurred. You approach the man and notice he is out of breath. He has what appears to be fresh bruising and cuts on his right knuckle. When you question him, you consider his answers to be quite curt. You do not like tattoos and your attention is drawn to the letters ACAB (all coppers are bastards) tattooed on his left knuckles. He says he was running for the bus, which leaves in five minutes. He says he is a building site worker, which is why his knuckle is cut. You check him on the Police National Computer and receive a response that he has previous convictions for assault. You interpret his demeanour as suspicious, and, along with his appearance and your PNC check, you arrest him on suspicion of assault.

- How have you evaluated the information to a point of arrest?

- Have you made a legitimate arrest? Justify your answer.

Sample answers are provided at the end of this book.

PROBLEM-ORIENTED POLICING: ASSESSMENT AND DECISION MAKING

THE SARA MODEL

Information assessment is not just about criminal intelligence. There is a wider requirement for community-based intelligence linked with a decision-making model, in order to implement recommendations or solutions to an identified problem extraneous to the criminal investigation sphere.

As the SARA model is discussed in *Criminology and Crime Prevention* in this book series, as well as in other sources (Burton and McGregor, 2018; College of Policing, 2022f), it is enough to acknowledge here that the acronym stands for information Scanning, Analysis, Response and Assessment and is recognised as a decision-making model used to provide solutions to bespoke or specific problems (College of Policing, 2022f). These are not necessarily criminal in nature and SARA could apply to any major or critical incident. It can be argued to be both an analysis model and a decision-making model, and really is an integration of both.

SARA can be used to identify recurring problems in an area, develop a working hypothesis to try and address the problem, develop an evidence-based plan and determine the effectiveness of any measures taken.

CRITICAL THINKING ACTIVITY 5.2

LEVEL 6

Imagine you are the Safer Neighbourhood Officer for a particular area where issues are being raised by residents regarding a late-night club which plays loud music and attracts hundreds of people each weekend. The club is only supposed to serve alcohol until midnight but parties seem to last well into the early hours. Recently there have been several instances of cars being broken into, damage caused to vehicles and property, at least five assaults (minor and serious) and general community harassment. No single person is identified as responsible. Rather the various incidents seem generally linked to the behaviour of people attending and leaving the late-night club venue.

- Having considered the information, is this an appropriate set of circumstances for deploying the SARA model? Explain your answer.

Sample answers are provided at the end of this book.

In developing any recommendations from intelligence, another model is available called PESTEL. It allows decision makers at a strategic level to analyse a particular issue, problem or situation using multiple lenses of political, economic, sociological, technological, environmental or legal aspects (Heldon, 2009). This can very much link in with the following section, which examines risk factors in intelligence, such as the community impact of action resulting from it. Other modes of analysis are available and some further reading on this subject is included at the end of this chapter.

RISK ASSESSMENTS AND COMMUNITY TENSIONS

Any information may carry a risk, which must be identified and made clear to those it is disseminated to. Risk can be exacerbated by the way information is originated. For example, it may come from a CHIS who is in a dangerous position, which is made worse if the information is used. Alternatively, at a police briefing it may be noted that an offender is considered violent or suspected of being armed (suggestions by supervisors that '*you can expect him to be violent*' or to '*resist arrest*' only serve to pre-condition officers to the expectation of violence and what they might do, rather than the officers being able to approach the subject objectively). There are various examples where risks have not been properly identified and a member of the public or police officer has been injured as a result.

The greatest risk can come from under-developed intelligence and any intervention(s) based upon it. Examples include the shooting of Stephen Waldorf in 1983, mistakenly shot multiple times by police for sitting in a similar car to an escaped fugitive; the shooting of Jean Charles de Menezes in 2005 (mistaken intelligence that he was a suicide bomber); or the various child abuse scandals in recent years where various children providing information about abuse were ignored.

Another aspect to consider is risk originating from any proposed action taken as a result of intelligence analysis and recommendations. For example, if an early morning raid is planned to arrest a community leader or leader of a mosque in a largely ethnically populated area, various questions need to be asked before deploying investigators to take action. What are the community tension indicators in the area? Would it be better to wait where possible to make a more low-key arrest? What will the anticipated reaction of the local community be, can it be assuaged and how will any flashpoints be dealt with?

Information and intelligence can never be separated from intervention, outcomes and individual or public reaction. They are also linked to media and political influence (consider terrorist events) and none of these factors should be allowed to pressure any investigator to take shortcuts which in the long term only usually lead to disastrous outcomes.

PUBLIC INTEREST IMMUNITY

This is always going to be a risk to the confidentiality of information and intelligence. A myth has developed within law enforcement agencies over the years that information held as intelligence is somehow not disclosable to the defence if a prosecution is sought and that a judge can be relied upon to protect the information under public interest immunity (PII). This simply means it is not in the public interest for the information to be revealed. All information in a police investigation is potentially disclosable under the Criminal Procedure and Investigations Act 1996 (see the *Police Procedure and Evidence in the Criminal Justice System* book in the series for an in-depth examination of the responsibilities under the Act). There is no guarantee that an item of intelligence will not be revealed at court if the judge decides that it is in the interests of justice. For that reason, this chapter has underpinned the need to be sanitary and clinical when submitting intelligence, always protecting the source where possible.

In short, a PII application will be made on behalf of the police if the prosecutor (CPS) has identified material which meets the disclosure test and is satisfied that releasing the material would create a real risk of serious prejudice. The disclosure test is objective and simply decides whether any information undermines the prosecution case or assists the defence.

The essential point is that information and its analysis within the intelligence system can be protected up to a point but if it has been acted upon, it could be tested in court, whether it is sensitive or not. This may mean, for example, that if a CHIS has facilitated the information and for some reason this becomes a point in court, then you will have a choice – expose the CHIS or cease the prosecution to protect the CHIS.

CRITICAL MINDSET

Critical thinking must be a necessary constant during information gathering, information analysis and intervention deployment of analysis outcomes. It is something which affects law enforcement investigations and incidents across a broad range of activities and is dealt with in other books within this series (see Spooner et al, 2022, Chapters 4 and 6).

Here it is sufficient to reiterate that critical thinking is an important constituent part of information analysis and is a necessary mindset for anyone involved in intelligence evaluation or assessment. Information must be viewed as dispassionately and objectively as possible. A critical thinking approach offers the most transparent and non-emotional outcome.

Reviewing information in any regard should be done objectively, with the main question being what is the information telling you? What does it mean? This should never be an automatic process. What we take for granted we never question and there are many examples where this has failed investigators.

As a bit of light relief to substantiate this point, let's examine whether we have all been lied to since we were born.

Since being children we have been told that there are seven days in a week, 365 and a quarter days in a year, which makes 52 weeks in a year. Every four years to account for the extra quarter day we have a leap year, which means every four years we have 366 days.

We are also told that mathematics cannot lie.

So, multiply 52 weeks by seven days and what do you get?

A total of 364! So where are the missing days? You must be younger than you think.

The point this makes is to question everything you are analysing no matter how insignificant and understand what you are looking at before making any conclusions.

CONCLUSION

This chapter has provided a brief introduction and overview of the world of intelligence analysis, including criminal and other operational policing spheres of work. It has provided strategies to use when you analyse and evaluate information (the Ten Commandments) and considered already-recognised models such as SARA and PESTEL. Handling and analysing information and intelligence is rarely without risk and this chapter builds upon Chapters 1 and 3 by examining elements of risk and bias and some of the pitfalls which can affect intelligence outcomes. The examples and activities in the chapter are designed to develop your critical thinking skills across policing issues and your ability to reflect on the points being considered. The objective is always to contribute to the enhancement of policing practice and policy.

SUMMARY OF KEY CONCEPTS

This chapter has discussed some of the following key concepts.

- Understanding the concept of the intelligence cycle.

- Understanding what each facet of the traditional intelligence cycle means and how it applies.

- The Ten Commandments to adhere to when evaluating information.

- Understanding the SARA model and recognising that other models such as PESTEL are available.

- Recognising risk and threat linked to intelligence.

- Consideration of outcomes as part of intelligence analysis.

- That intelligence is multifaceted and needs constant review, analysis, transparency and accuracy.

CHECK YOUR KNOWLEDGE

1. Name three of the Ten Commandments for evaluation of information.

2. What are the four aspects of the SARA model?

3. Name three forms of bias which intelligence analysts must be aware of.

4. Why does information need to be sanitised?

5. Describe the five points of the intelligence cycle given in this chapter.

Sample answers are provided at the end of this book.

FURTHER READING

BOOKS AND BOOK CHAPTERS

Garner, G and McGlynn, P (2019) *Intelligence Analysis Fundamentals*. Boca Raton, FL: CRC Press.
This book is a comprehensive introductory text to the world of intelligence and its analysis, although some of the terms used are militarily based.

Pease, B E (2019) *Leading Intelligence Analysis: Lessons from the CIA's Analytic Frontlines*. Los Angeles, CA: Sage.
This book presents a different aspect of analysis, viewed from the perspective of international operations and also the view that leading analysis is different to conducting analysis.

ARTICLES IN JOURNALS

Giangiuseppe, P (2023) Deciphering Intelligence Analysis: The Synthetic Nature of the Core Intelligence Function. *Intelligence and National Security*, 38(1): 128–42.
This article will help you think about what intelligence analysis actually is. The article is systematic in exploring the general nature of intelligence analysis and structuring sensory data.

WEBSITES

The College of Policing guidance can be found here: www.college.police.uk/app/intelligence-management/analysis/analytical-techniques
It provides an overview of some of the analytical techniques currently on the UK policing radar.

CHAPTER 6
INFORMATION MANAGEMENT, OTHER AGENCIES AND INDIVIDUAL RIGHTS

LEARNING OBJECTIVES

AFTER READING THIS CHAPTER YOU WILL BE ABLE TO:

⚙ manage large amounts of policing information and data;

⚙ present data and information in a clear and concise manner;

⚙ apply a systematic process to the recording and management of real-world or virtual data;

⚙ identify what a memorandum of understanding (MOU) is and when one is required;

⚙ understand how to deal with a Freedom of Information Act request from a member of the public.

INTRODUCTION

This chapter discusses the management of information and data in more depth. Previous chapters have explained the ways in which intelligence can be gathered, the pathways available to do so and the protections afforded by the law. This chapter demonstrates how to manage information and data in an investigation during all its stages and the need for a systematic approach to recording, assessing and identifying evidential or intervention opportunities from it. In the next evidence-based policing example, you will see how a routine arrest for what is considered a low-level offence can soon transmute into a complex inquiry and it may be up to you to manage the inquiry. The chapter then explains how the analysis of primary data can be presented and used to inform evidence-based policing practice.

EVIDENCE-BASED POLICING

THE OFFENDER AND THE MAP

Imagine there have been several thefts from motor vehicles in your area over the last 12 months. You arrive at the police station one morning to be allocated an arrest file which has been left by the night shift officers who arrested a man running from the scene of a theft from a motor vehicle. When searched, he had two items in his possession subsequently identified as being stolen from the car. He also had two other items which may be from another vehicle parked on the same street as the one on which the man was arrested. A section 18 search authority under the Police and Criminal Evidence Act 1984 is granted for you by the custody office inspector (allowing a search of the man's home address for evidence of this offence or similar offences).

On entering the bedroom of the premises, you find a map on the wall which contains over 70 crosses, all within the area where car thefts have occurred over the last year. The map is seized as an evidential exhibit. Because there are so many crosses on the map and you have no idea what may have been stolen, you decide to seize various exhibits from the flat which total over 200 items of property. When the man is interviewed, he admits that every time he broke into a car he marked the spot with a cross on his map. You now have to cross-reference the crosses to any reported theft from motor vehicles and you establish that from the crosses on the map, only 21 have apparently been reported to the police. Some of the exhibits you recovered during the search of the premises match items described in the reports. Forty-nine crosses remain unexplained, and you have a large quantity of exhibits seized from the flat to try and identify, all of which are a form of information. Your task is to assess and convert the information you have in the form of exhibits and crime reports (and the lack of them) into evidence. Eventually, all

70 crosses were identified plus 11 additional attempted thefts from motor cars which he had not bothered to put on his map.

This investigation involved using the information already in the possession of the police by:

- conducting house-to-house inquiries on the streets where the map showed a cross but for which no crime report could be found, a means to identify the remaining crosses and to identify any property stolen to cross-check it with items seized from the offender's home address;

- contacting the victims who had reported theft from their vehicles during the time frame and which were identified on crime reports against the crosses on the map;

- cross-checking items uplifted from the offender's home address which matched the description of property reported stolen at the time;

- holding an open day at the police station during which the remaining items seized from the man's address were displayed – all victims (those who had reported crimes and those who had not) were invited to attend to attempt to identify whether any property was theirs and provide a way to identify it as such;

- matching any unresolved forensic evidence to the offender.

To successfully resolve these lines of inquiry, the information needed to be effectively managed, a skill which is explained throughout this chapter.

Discussion in this chapter links in with the legislation previously considered in Chapter 2 by explaining how intelligence can be shared between agencies, what a memorandum of understanding is and how it can be used when agencies collaborate on an investigation to share intelligence. The Freedom of Information Act is considered in terms of applications for information requested by members of the public and how information and intelligence is stored and 'weeded' appropriately by police forces. This chapter expands on the continuing theme throughout the book concerning the rights of the individual matched against the state requirement to ensure investigators have sufficient powers to protect the public when gathering information. This is particularly apparent when dealing with investigations which integrate with the relatively new cyber pathways via the internet (addressing potential impacts of digital pathways on policing intelligence).

MANAGEMENT OF POLICE INFORMATION (MOPI)

Intelligence-led policing (see Chapter 3) means that information has become the currency of mainstream policing and must be handled robustly, transparently and effectively. The age of computerisation has exacerbated the need for a systematic approach to the management of information at all levels of policing. Computers and digitisation of information mean that it can be gathered more quickly and there is a wider access to material than ever before. As technology continues to advance, there can be no doubt that information management has become a crucial lynchpin to the success of police investigations, risk management and public safety.

All police forces have their own system for managing information which forms part of the National Intelligence Model (NIM) and, if you become a police officer, it will depend on where you work as to the system nuances you will face. The NIM structure will remain the same nationally but system nuances and force preferences may differ slightly in the way intelligence is numbered, analysed and managed. This is usually because of resources available and the budget limitations which all police forces constantly face. Therefore, this section concentrates on ways to manage information in investigations rather than intelligence offices, a situation faced at some point by all police investigators.

POLICING SPOTLIGHT

Imagine you are an investigator who is seconded to an incident room investigating serious and organised crime resulting in a murder. A meeting of two gangs was arranged using social media but it so far remains unclear who was the organiser(s). Over 20 arrests have been made, which means that multiple addresses have been searched. The incident room is in relation to a gang fight on waste ground in your area, where one of the protagonists was shot and killed. All exhibits which have so far been seized from various addresses have been carefully logged by an appointed exhibits officer (responsible for all material seized as part of the investigation). Due to the circumstances of the crime, 17 search warrants have so far been executed and all electronic equipment capable of internet chat has been taken possession of by the police. All the items must now be assessed for information and evidence and interrogated for information which will lead to evidence relevant to the murder and any gang activity concerning drugs, which is believed to have been the reason for the two sides meeting in the first place. The firearm used in the murder is also still missing. The best way to systematically manage information on this scale, including the tracking of exhibits sent to and from forensic computer analysis or for other testing, is to include all relevant details in a spreadsheet (see Table 6.1).

Table 6.1 Spreadsheet example

Item number	Date of seizure	Exhibit reference	Description	Time and place seized	Owner	Priority	Reason for seizure	Date to high-tech crime	Examined by and statement	Date from high-tech crime	Evidence retrieved	Witness statement for audit trail
1	26/03/2022	CIH/1	Apple laptop computer, on when uplifted	0810, front bedroom, 123 ABC Street, Nottingham off study desk	Henry Jade (12/10/01), 123 ABC Street, Nottm	Not urgent	Henry Jade on periphery of gang. Computer seized as he is a gang member known to be at the scene of the night of the shooting.					
2	26/03/2022	DWC/1	Xbox	0900, downstairs front living room, 345 Kenny Street, Nottingham	Jonah Heston (26/08/02), 345 Kenny Street, Nottm	Urgent	Jonah Heston is described by witnesses to the shooting to have snatched the shotgun used in the shooting after it had been fired and left the scene. Weapon still missing.	28/03/2022	pending	pending	pending	pending

For anything other than major incidents such as murder investigations (where a Home Office Large Major Enquiry System, HOLMES II, would be deployed – see the section later in the chapter), the simplest way to record large amounts of information is to use a spreadsheet. Using a program like Microsoft Excel, which all police forces have access to, means you will be able to add as many exhibits and vertical columns as you need. This is a very useful facility in an ongoing investigation.

A spreadsheet such as this is straightforward to create. Basic details such as times, dates and descriptions simply need entering into the appropriate column. In this example, suppose that the Xbox exhibit had been forensically interrogated and further information discovered in its chat facility. That information would simply be entered into the spreadsheet, as well as including a note as to whether the new information had been submitted back into the NIM for the investigation and whether it had been further acted upon.

Imagine 600 electronic exhibits being listed and interrogated using this recording method. Not only does the spreadsheet keep track of exhibits, the information, relevant times, days and dates and so on, but it can also be used to keep track of exhibits which will be used in the investigation, whether witness statements have been submitted for each item and the priority status of remaining items. These aspects tie in with disclosure requirements under the Criminal Procedure and Investigations Act 1996, which accounts for all information collected during an investigation. In effect, the working spreadsheet becomes a library of material relevant or non-relevant to the investigation and any subsequent prosecution. As each exhibit is interrogated, it can also be used to record what information has been extracted and any intelligence potential it contains. Spreadsheets can be as small or as large as required and in each section you can include as much detail as you think is relevant. In any subsequent review of material at any stage, the spreadsheet will act as an easily checkable repository of information. It, or parts of it, can also be produced in court if required.

PRESENTING INFORMATION AND INTELLIGENCE

It can be difficult to present information in a clear and concise manner if there is a lot of it. You may be able to manage it well using the spreadsheet example in Figure 6.1 but presenting the salient points clearly in meetings or briefings presents another problem entirely. Various programs exist whereby information and intelligence can be presented using a chart: in essence, drawing a picture. Such programs tend to be privately developed and licensed for law enforcement to use, the one used by most UK police forces being I2. This allows simple to complex investigations to be pictorially represented. The program uses a broad series of picture icons to enable any operation to be charted and allows complex inquiries to be represented in a straightforward manner. This can be a great advantage to an investigator who has to brief senior officers or prosecutors or anyone else who may have no previous knowledge of the case. Charts can even be used in court to ensure complex cases can be easily understood by jurors. Consider the following intelligence information in the next critical thinking activity.

CRITICAL THINKING ACTIVITY 6.1

LEVEL 4

Imagine you are conducting a human trafficking case and are asked to brief senior officers regarding the current stage of investigation. You have established that a particular individual, a male, is the main facilitator of the trafficking and he uses three internet sites to recruit individuals from Romania, persuading them there is a better life in the UK. Intelligence from the websites suggests that six companies are involved in the money laundering side of his business, four of which are in the UK, one in Cyprus and the remaining one in Romania. Funds appear to travel away from the UK to Cyprus, through Romania, only to return through one of the businesses and into the pockets of the man behind all six companies. The offender uses four addresses in your area to house people he has trafficked and uses them as employees for a chicken factory (Poultry for You) 20 miles away.

If you attempted to relay this information at a management or tasking meeting, it is likely that most people present would quickly become lost in the text and would not really follow the salient points. If you draw it, however, the information becomes clear and simple to follow. This is where the I2 program is versatile. Behind each icon is an unlimited data field, so the program can be used as a database of the entire investigation for intelligence handling as well as charting.

* Try drawing this information in picture format to make your briefing easier to follow.

Sample answers are provided at the end of this book.

INFORMATION FOR POLICE PURPOSES

Remember that all information for police purposes is covered by the General Data Protection Regulations 2018 (see Chapter 2). The National Centre for Policing Excellence (2005b, p 6) set out what this means, police purposes being described as:

* *protecting life and property;*

* *preserving order;*

- *preventing the commission of offences;*

- *bringing offenders to justice; and*

- *any duty or responsibility of the police arising from common law or statute law.*

In other words, *everything.*

Anyone engaged in police information management must now be trained so there is a baseline of consistency in standards across the UK police service. Information from police systems must never be accessed for personal reasons or purposes.

REFLECTIVE PRACTICE 6.1

LEVEL 5

INFORMATION SCENARIO 1

PC Donaldson is in the process of moving house and when he last visited the new premises he has bought, he noticed three men working on a car engine that had been removed and placed on the driveway of the property. The men looked to be in their mid-thirties and were scruffy in appearance. This bothered PC Donaldson for a few days, and he started to worry about noise levels and car parts making the view from his new house unsightly. After two or three days, PC Donaldson completed a few basic checks on the property and established who owned the house with the car engine. He then checked the individual on the Police National Computer and satisfied himself there was no trace of criminality next to his new house.

INFORMATION SCENARIO 2

PC Smith is on duty when called to a fight in the street. On arrival it is clear that the fight has escalated into a larger brawl and may even be a violent disorder situation (Public Order Act 1986). Other units arrive and although tensions remain high and two cars are burning in the road, PC Smith realises his partner will shortly be travelling through the area to get home. PC Smith rings his partner from his radio, informs them of the street situation and suggests a different route home be taken.

- Reflect upon the actions of the officers in these two scenarios. Do you think they acted correctly or not? Justify and explain your answers.

Sample answers are provided at the end of this book.

INFORMATION SHARING

This generally operates on two levels, nationally within the UK and internationally. Information sharing can take place in several ways, involving two agencies or multiple agencies, or even within different parts of the same organisation. It is well documented in the policing litera-ture and general media that poor information handling has led to certain notorious offenders and criminality remaining undetected despite the knowledge or evidence required in the investigation already being in police hands (for example, the Yorkshire Ripper investigation, Soham murders, Levi Bellfield murders, Pembrokeshire murders – offender John Cooper). In each case, mishaps, ignorance or system issues in handling information delayed the arrest of the offender and possibly cost lives as a result, particularly where more than one police force was involved. For example, in the Soham murders, the subsequent Bichard Inquiry (2004) identified that the police and the social services in Humberside treated the case independently (separately). This resulted in the ineffective sharing of informa-tion, particularly between social services and the police. In turn, this was exacerbated by Humberside Police's failure in the way their intelligence systems were managed in the case, a point admitted in the inquiry by the then Chief Constable.

The ensuing Bichard Inquiry Report (2004) in which 36 separate recommendations were made can be found in full at https://dera.ioe.ac.uk/6394/1/report.pdf.

It is vital to have a systematic approach to information handling but in investigation circles it is just as important to be able to share information. There are several ways of accomplishing this while still complying with the Data Protection Act 2018 and other relevant legislation. The central tenet is that exchanging any police information must be lawful and for a policing purpose (College of Policing, 2020) and must also comply with the principles of the NIM (see Chapter 5).

MEMORANDUM OF UNDERSTANDING (MOU)

These are quite common agreements between different agencies. An MOU is not a con-tract but it specifies what the agreement is about, why it has been made and precisely what the expectations are of each party to it. It also establishes the guidelines for the col-laboration and the level of commitment from each participating agency (Guidetti, 2009). A myth has developed in some areas of law enforcement that if an MOU is in place, it makes data sharing lawful and without restriction. This is erroneous and, to support data sharing of personal information where an MOU is in place, an additional information sharing agreement (ISA) is also required (College of Policing, 2020). It is the ISA which allows the data sharing to take place.

INFORMATION SHARING AGREEMENT (ISA)

Unlike the MOU which explains the working relationship and expectations of each signatory to it, an ISA should define the extent of the information to be shared and the lawful basis for doing so. MOUs and ISAs tend to be used by officers in specialist units where liaison with other agencies is quite frequent. They are quite rare where uniform patrol duties are concerned.

Consider the following example.

CRITICAL THINKING ACTIVITY 6.2

LEVEL 4

As a result of a foreign national escaping from the control of a modern slavery and human trafficking organised crime group, a charity supporting the individual makes a complaint of trafficking to the police. During the early stages of the investigation, it becomes very clear that multiple agencies will need to be approached in order to gain information, process intelligence and pursue a prosecution.

- What do you think happened in this example?

Sample answers are provided at the end of this book.

Where multiple agencies are involved, there are three key requirements for consideration when creating an ISA.

1. What needs to be shared?

2. What is the purpose of sharing the data and could the intended result be achieved without doing so?

3. Is there any risk to the institution or to any individual if the data is shared?

PROJECT MANAGEMENT

We have established that any data forming part of the intelligence and evidential remit of an investigation can be shared in certain circumstances, usually by the mechanisms explained above. These aspects integrate with the overall project management of larger investigations which may have policy, strategic, tactical and investigative levels, all dealing with the same information. It is therefore imperative that effective project management is in place. It is great having information, data and intelligence available but, if it is not effectively integrated into the whole project, it is all for nothing. This is important in your own investigations but even more so when collaborative working is involved.

Table 6.2 Checklist of key areas for working collaboratively

Media strategy	This can apply in complex cases or at routine level (perhaps a crime such as a rape has been committed and the public need to be warned). It is usually the remit of a senior officer but even at routine level you may find yourself approached by members of the media or press. As a general rule, it is a good idea to direct any such approach to your force press office.
Application of information-gathering methods	Decide what you are going to do and the methods which you will try first. Remember the menu of tactics for information gathering (see Chapter 4).
Tasking and co-ordination	You need to consider all elements of information gathered, intelligence gleaned and its effective application to achieve the aims and objectives of the investigation or collaborative working (including the legislative legalities of work undertaken).
Risk assessment	Continual risk assessment is required for all aspects of the investigation, in particular any risks to CHIS elements, covert surveillance, open-source intelligence sweeps and other information-gathering methods.
Investigation plan	The intelligence aspect is a large part of any investigation and needs constant updating to ensure effective investigation based upon information learned in the course of an inquiry.
Clear communications	Essential if all parties to an investigation or joint working project are to work effectively. Each investigator, intelligence operative or collaborative partner needs to constantly be aware of the direction of the investigation, what they are tasked with and why, and of any changes in the imperatives of an inquiry in order to avoid duplication, resource wastage and intelligence overlap.
Evaluation	All aspects of an investigation or collaborative project should be constantly reviewed. A good way to achieve continuity of evaluation is to set milestones where reviews can be conducted, data drawn together and decisions made to take the process forwards.
Stakeholders	Ensure all stakeholders know exactly what is expected of them during the investigation or joint working. There is no point in several units or investigators trying to uncover the same information or conducting the same inquiries.

An easy way to remember these points is to apply the mnemonic MATRICES.

HOME OFFICE LARGE MAJOR ENQUIRY SYSTEM (HOLMES)

This is an incident information management system (particularly for murder incidents) that is nationally recognised and deployed by all police forces across the UK. Not only can it be used to record all information gathered as part of a major investigation, but it is also designed to cross-reference it as well to ensure nothing is missed. The system was designed as one of the long-standing outcomes of the Yorkshire Ripper case (murders between 1975 and 1980 in West Yorkshire and other northern counties). It was a case severely criticised for the way in which information was (badly) handled and, during which, the offender, Peter Sutcliffe, was interviewed nine times. Without an information management system in this case (such as HOLMES), the inquiry was overwhelmed. For example, 250,000 people were interviewed, 32,000 witness statements taken and over five million car registrations checked (Mason, 2020).

Thanks to the internet it is now possible for police forces to link incidents in appropriate circumstances, although it remains the decision of each police force as to which major investigations (aside from murders) HOLMES is used for (CPS, 2021). Tools included within HOLMES include document storage and a host of categories into which information can be inputted, uniquely numbered and recalled at the touch of a button. If the system is used properly and effectively, the volume of information gathered on any major incident can be effectively and easily managed. In turn, this should prevent duplication of inquiries as well as the ability to maintain an overview of intelligence needs and parameters alongside evidential gathering and disclosure that may be being made.

In an age of digitisation and the continuing expansion of the internet there are many products now on the market, all of which can be easily located online. Any system used in policing needs to have the principles of effective and lawful data collection, a facility to store and manage documents, an analysis capability, effective online security and data-sharing facilities. An additional consideration, of course, is the ability of any system to be used in compliance with the prevailing laws of any country it is used within. In the UK this means (among others) the Human Rights Act 1998, Criminal Procedure and Investigations Act 1996, Police and Criminal Evidence Act 1984, Investigatory Powers Act 2016, Regulation of Investigatory Powers Act 2000 and the Data Protection Acts 1998 and 2018 including GDPR.

FREEDOM OF INFORMATION ACT 2000 (FOI) AND CRIMINAL PROCEDURE AND INVESTIGATIONS ACT 1996 (CPIA – DISCLOSURE)

These two pieces of legislation are very important when you think about the information, data or intelligence you might find yourself managing and responsible for.

When dealing with information within a police force, you need to be aware that members of the public are entitled under the Freedom of Information Act 2000 to make a request for information. The request must be in writing, including by electronic means as well as on paper (FOI 2000, s.8). It may not only concern a case or an individual but can also include information about systems, procedures or results. If there is an excessive cost involved in producing the information or it requires too much data, the request can be denied. In certain instances, the applicant may receive a refusal but with a proviso that if the applicant wants to pay those costs, then it may still be furnished. There are of course other safeguards to any request made and these include where information is subject to a criminal or civil investigation or proceedings, or where it is obtained from confidential sources. The point is to be aware that it is possible for information to find its way into the public domain if data is mishandled or legislation is not understood or adhered to. FOI requests in some cases even include emails sent between staff which may mention the specific information being sought.

REFLECTIVE PRACTICE 6.2

LEVEL 5

STUDENT RESEARCH

Imagine you are a student writing a research paper or completing a dissertation for an independent study, the subject of which is how many cash detentions have been made by officers in your area under the Proceeds of Crime Act 2002. You may have already conducted primary research into cash detention (a method of taking money from suspects which has originated from criminal activity or is suspected of being about to be used in criminal activity) using a survey or interviews. This has left you with questions unanswered by

→

your data about the number of cash seizures made, the number that successfully resulted in court action and the number returned to individuals without prosecution.

- Can you submit an FOI request to ask for the information you suspect is held by the police force in question or do you need more information in these circumstances?

Sample answers are provided at the end of this book.

We know from Chapter 6 of the *Police Procedure and Evidence in the Criminal Justice System* book that as a police investigator at all levels you must bear in mind that any information obtained in the course of an investigation is potentially disclosable under the disclosure of information rules (CPIA 1996). CPIA is comprehensively dealt with in another book in this series, *Police Procedure and Evidence in the Criminal Justice System*, but the focus here is in respect of police intelligence handling. Although a myth has developed that intelligence items entered in the NIM are completely protected, under CPIA 1996 this is not necessarily the case. Accurate recording of information across policing is necessary not only for intervention opportunities (arrests, searches and so on) to be created, but also for prosecution cases to be successful by properly adhering to disclosure rules in a transparent and ordered manner.

The underlying point is that the focus tends to be on how the police manage large quantities of information, but it is equally (and practically) important for intelligence managers and staff to monitor how intelligence is fed into the NIM. The two aspects are connected and as the goal is usually to successfully prosecute an offender, a weather eye should always be kept on how information is written and what the effect would be if certain information did end up being disclosed to the defendant or in court (see Chapter 5).

Be careful how you use information systems, particularly in dealing with intelligence, and think about what you are writing. Nothing is 100 per cent protected.

CRITICAL THINKING ACTIVITY 6.3

LEVEL 5

Imagine you are working in the force data protection office when two Freedom of Information Act 2000 requests are received by email.

REQUEST 1

The request states that information is requested about a drugs arrest made in the city centre in your area leading to the arrest of three people for drug trafficking. You research the case with the Crown Prosecution Service and find it is listed for a Crown Court hearing in six months' time.

REQUEST 2

The request asks how many times cash has been seized in your county area, how many times the Police and Criminal Evidence Act 1984 was used, when the proceeds of crime element was instigated to make the seizure into a cash detention, how many cases were successful in court, what the failure rate of cases is and how many money laundering charges linked to cash seizures have been successfully prosecuted.

- What do you think about these two requests?

- From what you have read so far do you think they are reasonable requests?

- Do you think they have to be complied with?

Sample answers are provided at the end of this book.

END-POINT RISKS TO INFORMATION

Intelligence items are not usually introduced in court or as part of the prosecution bundle but there have been cases where certain items have been ordered to be released by court judges. The underlying rule is always to be aware that the way in which information is obtained, written and processed may at some point come under scrutiny. If any judge orders information to be disclosed because of an application to the court by a defence barrister, there will be very little you will be able to do about it unless it falls within the scope of public interest immunity (see Chapter 5). Your prosecutor may appeal such an order but the judge's word is final. Here are four important tips when dealing with intelligence submissions.

1. Be careful how information is submitted.

2. Be clear in what is written.

3. Be as accurate with your information as you can be.

4. Sanitise any information which may lead to witnesses, victims or CHIS being identified.

You should be able to see that there is a parallel between law enforcement information and intelligence management and academic research management. In the following example, consider the four intelligence tips in relation to managing a university research project.

REFLECTIVE PRACTICE 6.3

LEVEL 6

- Compare your thoughts about what is required when you gather information for an essay or a project at university or college with what is required for an investigation.

The four points remain the same. What you learn in critical thinking and research ability as a student become transferable skills relevant to policing.

Think about a dissertation project.

First of all, you would conduct a review of available literature and you would carefully examine the information. Universities expect you to explain in a clear and cogent fashion what you have found in that review before you conduct any primary research.

You will ensure accuracy in how you collect your data and transparent in your analysis about any recommendations resulting from it.

Finally, throughout the project you will have managed your information sources to keep track of references and material used and you will anonymise any primary research data you have collected so as not to identify any participating individual or organisation.

At all stages you would employ a critical thinking approach to ascertain what the information is telling you, just as you would if you were establishing the provenance of one or multiple intelligence items.

The approaches used to manage research project information and intelligence information are therefore very similar in many aspects.

An important point to understand from this reflective exercise is that when you are conducting an intelligence operation or a research project, this is a transferable skill which is just as relevant to policing as it is to research and business.

DIGITAL ENVIRONMENT IMPLICATIONS

The internet is now ever present in all our lives and is largely beneficial for us all. Recovering information from within it is really no different than any other form of policing except for speed and the volume of data you are to search through. In investigation terms it offers the potential for a wealth of information to be gathered, often in a short space of time. One of the fundamental issues if the internet is to be used in an investigation is to establish an audit trail for that information. There is no guarantee that a website which is in existence one day will still be there the next. This makes it even more important that information is saved from the screens when it is accessed, timed and dated as usual and recorded in accordance with the rules of evidence. The difference is the volume of information you can sort through in a shorter space of time.

A practical tip when using a spreadsheet is to have it open when you are interrogating web pages for information, meaning you can record the data contemporaneously so that the audit trail always remains clear and you avoid a backlog which can cause a severe drain on your time. Once you establish the habit, it will become second nature.

CONCLUSION

This chapter has considered why information needs to be effectively managed and has provided you with methods to deal with large amounts of data. It has equipped you with strategies to record information in a way that is ordered, transparent and accessible. Project management of large quantities of information has been explained using the mnemonic MATRICES, a tool which can be applied to any large information undertaking. Risks to data have been approached from two different aspects. First, the opportunity afforded to the general public to make applications for information. Second, from the perspective of the end-point risk to data, and how information might be released by a court notwithstanding any protection afforded in the prosecution case until that point is reached. Information requires precise and careful handling and all of the above will facilitate effective data handling and management, always with the aim of improving evidence-based policing, policy which drives it and the translation of reliable methods into effective and routine intelligence management practice.

SUMMARY OF KEY CONCEPTS

This chapter has discussed some of the following key concepts.

⚙ Why information must be managed efficiently and transparently and how to do so logically and efficiently.

→

⚙ How to effectively manage information in any policing inquiry by being logical and systematic. Develop your own system if necessary to include core data to assist information retrieval no matter what the scale of inquiry.

⚙ Parallels between intelligence information management and academic research information management. There is no real difference and the skill in doing one is transferable to the other.

⚙ The accessibility of information by outside sources using the Freedom of Information Act 2000. Be alert that not only you can apply to public bodies for information. So can members of the public and, of course, so can the criminals.

⚙ The component parts of collaborative working, project management and managing information across multiple agencies.

⚙ Risk to information when cases reach court. Be alert to the pitfalls which can derail a case, especially where CHIS are concerned.

⚙ How to present information, including in pictorial form. Be simple and precise as your information may have to be presented to a jury who have no knowledge of policing intelligence practices.

⚙ Implications for data management, involving the digital environment. Understand the implications of the digital environment and figure out how investigations might be affected.

CHECK YOUR KNOWLEDGE

1. Why is a MOPI system required?

2. Which police purposes are covered by the General Data Protection Regulations 2018?

3. What is a memorandum of understanding (MOU) and when should it be used?

4. What is an information sharing agreement (ISA)?

5. What does the mnemonic MATRICES stand for?

Sample answers are provided at the end of this book.

FURTHER READING

BOOKS AND BOOK CHAPTERS

Bilton, M (2012) *Wicked Beyond Belief: The Hunt for the Yorkshire Ripper*. London: Harper Press.
This is an award-winning book which explores the Yorkshire Ripper case and details the problems with the volume of information and lack of an effective information management structure (in the days pre-internet).

Buckley, J (2014) *Managing Intelligence: A Guide for Law Enforcement Professionals*. Oxford: Routledge.
This book deals with intelligence management from an international perspective (including the UK). It encourages you to appreciate that some of the inhibitors, processes, issues and problems surrounding the intelligence theatre of policing and the way intelligence is managed are quite similar.

James, A (2016) *Understanding Police Intelligence Work*. Bristol: Policy Press.
This book explains how intelligence has developed in policing over recent years and how the intelligence architecture has modernised to make its governance more effective. From a digital environment perspective, the book considers the current risk and threat environment and how 'Big Data' is emerging.

ARTICLES IN JOURNALS

Bell, P, Dean, G, and Gottschalk, P (2010) Information Management in Law Enforcement: The Case of Police Intelligence Strategy Implementation. *International Journal of Information Management*, 30(4): 343–9.
This article considers information handling from a strategic aspect.

WEBSITES

The College of Policing guidance about management of information can be found here: www.college.police.uk/app/information-management/information-sharing

SAMPLE ANSWERS

CHAPTER 1

CRITICAL THINKING ACTIVITY 1.1

The conversation with the dog walker has produced information at this stage. It is not, by itself, intelligence. Information needs to be checked and corroborated before it is acted upon, which is why the intelligence cycle (see Chapter 5) was designed. Questions which would test the details you have received could include the following.

- Is the farmer called Jackson?

- Does he own the farm?

- Has he previously been in trouble with the police?

- If so, was the offending concerned with handling stolen goods?

- Do any of his known associates have recent entries on the intelligence system in your force area?

REFLECTIVE PRACTICE 1.1

Whenever you deal with different agencies in your policing career, it is always wise to check how they define and use intelligence as the intelligence architecture and its purpose may vary. This reflective practice activity is simply to remind you not to take the word 'intelligence' at face value, nor to presume that everyone understands it to be the same thing. Intelligence handling is about critical thinking, not accepting things at face value, and if you are aware of differences from the outset, you will avoid the pitfalls of making assumptions.

POLICING SPOTLIGHT: KNOWING THE RISKS

It is important that you take care of information, handle it securely and never put yourself in the position where you potentially expose documents or data to the risk of compromise (where it can be accessed, leaked, copied or stolen).

Always use a secure work laptop.

Never take paperwork home.

Never put data on an unprotected flash drive.

CRITICAL THINKING ACTIVITY 1.2

The considerations here are as follows.

- The large amount of money in several accounts, only two of which are in the suspect's name.

- Two accounts are held abroad in Europe.

- Passports found in different names concealed to avoid discovery.

- Blank birth certificates.

- The nature of the investigation has changed and the new information/evidence you have found could escalate the NIM level to 2 or 3. It may key into a regional or national inquiry, may be terrorist or human trafficking (or other offence) related and has international aspects already (two bank accounts abroad).

- It is very likely this would escalate to at least a regional, if not an international one, so level 2 or 3 could now apply. Investigation is never predictable, and cases can escalate or de-escalate at a moment's notice.

CRITICAL THINKING ACTIVITY 1.3

The offence was committed between 0330 and 0400 hours. You observed John Smith driving the BMW motor car approximately one mile from the scene of the burglary at 0405 hours. You also observed a long scratch in the yellow paintwork of the rear offside passenger door of the vehicle. Yellow paint was found on the gatepost of the building where the burglary took place. Smith is known to have previous convictions for night-time offences. In this scenario, what may have been diligent observation and a routine intelligence 'sighting' can be processed into usable intelligence. The information you have provided can be matched against the details of the burglary to provide reasonable suspicion that Smith was involved in the offending. This may well result in a search warrant at Smith's home address and his arrest on suspicion of burglary. You never know when what you see will be useful. You are a cog in an intelligence wheel you cannot see but which, without your input, cannot be effective.

REFLECTIVE PRACTICE 1.2

All of the things you have been ordered to do in this example are extremely intrusive. If you were to carry out such actions without legislative, supervisory and sometimes judicial oversight, it would be a massive infringement of the individual's civil and human rights. In the past, it is arguable that such actions, if not overseen correctly, led to miscarriages of justice and abuse of police powers (see the Radcliffe-on-Soar power station case: www.theguardian.com/environment/2011/jan/10/activists-undercover-officer-mark-kennedy). This in turn led to a massive public outcry about using undercover police officers.

The public need to be assured that 'Big Brother' is not watching them unlawfully and there must always be a balance between state power and individual rights.

CRITICAL THINKING ACTIVITY 1.4

EXAMPLE 1

The answer is 'No'. Mr Smith is not a CHIS. He offers information on one occasion only and he is not covertly operating for the police in any way. If Mr Smith was directed to find out more about Fox, then he may become a CHIS if he operates covertly in doing so and if he forms relationships which would navigate him nearer to information sources concerning Fox.

EXAMPLE 2

On the first occasion Audrey provides information she is not a CHIS. She is acting as a responsible citizen. When she is re-contacted and asked to find out more information, she is now being directed to act covertly and is likely at that point to be considered a CHIS. In reality, her details would be passed to a CHIS handling unit to ascertain how she could be deployed and to define the parameters of an official CHIS relationship.

REFLECTIVE PRACTICE 1.3

In this instance it could be construed that by visiting the website three times for information, you may be engaging in surveillance. This is a grey area but one which you need to be aware of when searching for internet information linked to investigations. It may also impact on disclosure because, in theory, you should print each screen to prove an audit trail for any evidence you later use as a result of what you find.

CRITICAL THINKING ACTIVITY 1.5

In Example 1 you would apply parts 3, 4, 5 and 6 of the Six-Step Framework. You already have the first two under consideration. Your aim would be to corroborate anything you had been told. The obvious starting point would be the Cat and Pigeon pub. The landlord corroborates that Brian and Billy were in the pub as Brian had told you. Billy had mentioned during a previous drinking session that he drank at another pub in a suburb south of the city. It was named after a soldier and is near a church. This pub was identified within a matter of hours and visited. The landlord knew Billy and thought he lived a couple of streets away. House to house established there was a Billy at a particular premises. Billy answered the door and immediately admitted 'she's *in the back room*'.

This is a real example and by starting at the pub, ten hours later the address of Billy was identified, and a woman's body was found in the back room of the premises. She had been dead for about six weeks. Just because a witness sounds fanciful does not mean that what you are being told is not true. Objectivity and thoroughness are necessary at all times, particularly when dealing with a vulnerable individual like Brian.

Example 2 requires all of the Six-Step Framework to be applied. This is based on the true story of Professor Boris Rankov, who decided to investigate the legend of the Greek trireme to prove or disprove it once and for all. Bearing in mind the event was 2000 years ago, he started by first identifying all texts which mentioned the trireme. He then examined thousands of pottery shards worldwide to see if any drawings of such ships had survived. He processed the information until he had enough intelligence for an out-come. He persuaded the Greek government to fund his research so that he could build a trireme from specifications painstakingly worked out from literature and pottery. The result was that the ship was built against all the odds and was sea-trialled at the Greek naval school on Poros in 1985.

CHECK YOUR KNOWLEDGE

1. Intelligence is produced when information is passed through a process (usually the intelligence cycle) so it can be developed to be used tactically or strategically for an outcome.

2. (i) Information which already exists; (ii) information generated by law enforcement; and (iii) information from witnesses or victims.

3. Level 1 – local level; level 2 – regional level; and level 3 – national and international.

4.

    i. Identify sources.

    ii. Gather information.

    iii. Establish the reliability of your sources.

    iv. Corroborate your sources.

    v. Analyse any information you uncover and create actionable intelligence (commonly referred to as the intelligence cycle; see Chapter 5).

    vi. Utilise the intelligence to identify an intervention point (produce an outcome).

5. Covert human intelligence source.

CHAPTER 2

CRITICAL THINKING ACTIVITY 2.1

This is a famous paragraph from the work of Blackstone (1778). It sums up how a society should function. Society (the whole) protects its citizens, and each part of the whole (each citizen) surrenders certain freedoms (obeying the laws which the society makes and adheres to) as a tradeoff for the protection offered by the state (the whole). Anyone not obeying the laws of the whole (society) will have to live outside that state protection – outside the law, which is where the term outlaw comes from.

Blackstone is important because creating and enforcing legislation to govern and protect citizens has to be a delicate balance between the needs of the state (the country) and its population (each individual). This is why laws governing the extent to which the state can intervene in a citizen's private life are essential. When there is an imbalance then a dictatorship or public violence can ensue. Blackstone is the foundation for legislation such as the Human Rights Act 1998 (see the evidence-based policing example) and the articles which protect the rights of private citizens against unnecessary intrusion from government or law enforcement.

REFLECTIVE PRACTICE 2.1

Although PC Brian may be using his initiative, which all police officers are encouraged to do, he may, in his enthusiasm to impress CID, have forgotten (or is unaware) that to check the same premises several times every day may be argued to be surveillance. Therefore, an application under RIPA could be required. By undertaking unilateral action, despite his good intentions, PC Brian may well be jeopardising the investigation being carried out by CID, possibly without even knowing he is doing so.

CRITICAL THINKING ACTIVITY 2.2

Alternative thinking can be very useful when any policing investigation does not produce the expected result. The officer in this (real-life) example was aware that to breed over five litters of dogs a year, a dog breeding licence is required. Because the Proceeds of Crime Act 2002 (POCA) applies to regulatory offences as well as criminal offences, then any money the man had made from the dog breeding without a licence could be classed as originating from an offence (failing to have a dog breeding licence). A cash seizure under POCA of all of the money was made and the man in real life was charged with two offences: money laundering and breeding dogs without a licence. He pleaded guilty to both offences at the magistrates' court and lost all of the money, which was forfeited by the court. Without the use of the dog breeding and money laundering offences, the drug raid would not have yielded a positive result against a known organised crime group. This example demonstrates that thorough knowledge of a target premises is required. The dog compound in this case was large and clearly visible from the air. The helicopter crew had only been briefed to check for a heat source which may indicate a cannabis grow. Like the officers initially at the search premises, they were unaware of possibilities concerning unlawful breeding; thus, options to resolve the investigation were unintentionally limited by not gathering and considering all options offered by the known pre-search-warrant information.

REFLECTIVE PRACTICE 2.2

This is an example where knowledge of powers will lead to a better result. In this case of domestic violence, not only can the offender be convicted of the assault but, if any of the investigators are aware of the Powers of Criminal Courts Act, the court can be asked at the time of conviction to disqualify the offender from driving and for this disqualification to run consecutive to (after) his prison sentence. As he used his car to drive to commit the assault in the first instance, information has now been received from the neighbour that he will reoffend when the Crown Court case is over. The information from the neighbour can be made into actionable intelligence simply by making the request to the sentencing court. This can only be done if investigators are aware of these powers which, unfortunately, is not always the case (Hughes, 2021). Two important points are made here. First, that information can be useful at any stage of an investigation, even during or after a court case or conviction. Second, that some powers are forgotten about or overlooked but are ones which can enhance outcomes and offer additional possibilities when one conclusion seems the only one available.

CRITICAL THINKING ACTIVITY 2.3

Coercion or bribery can never be used by the UK police to gain information or evidence to be used or relied upon in any investigation. In this example you should bring the request to the attention of a supervisor and refrain from becoming involved in what is clearly a coercive attempt to force someone to inform for the police. This is aside from any police discipline offences which may be committed in such a situation.

CRITICAL THINKING ACTIVITY 2.4

Your action in carving a small line into the shoe of the offender might have resulted in information to afford an intervention opportunity (an arrest) but you have acted unlawfully, transgressing the RIPA and human rights legislation. You have also transgressed the Police and Criminal Evidence Act. You can never take matters into your own hands to generate unlawful intelligence. Work within the legal parameters – it may take slightly longer but information correctly obtained is worth waiting for.

CRITICAL THINKING ACTIVITY 2.5

PC Smithson may actually be acting unlawfully and there have been several cases where companies have sued the police because false identities have been used without authority and the knowledge of the individual involved. In a US case, a woman found out that a federal agency had used her photograph and other details to create a false identity to converse with several criminals. She successfully sued the US Justice Department and was awarded $134,000 in damages (Lyons, 2015). In the UK, it is likely that a RIPA

2000 authority for such an online identity would have to be considered and applied for to allow such action to be taken. It is unlikely that an individual's actual details would be used. The ethics of using fake online profiles is still being debated (this is one of the considerations of the Online Safety Bill which, at time of writing, is passing through the House of Lords and is at the committee stage of the process).

CHECK YOUR KNOWLEDGE

1. Regulation of Investigatory Powers Act (2000).

2. Powers of Criminal Courts (Sentencing) Act 2000.

3. The aim is to be transparent in policing and avoid pitfalls and shortcuts that may lead to corrupt behaviour or miscarriages of justice.

4. Any information which the bank feels is relevant to suspicious activity.

5. (i) Surface web; (ii) deep web; and (iii) dark web.

6. Computer Misuse Act 1990.

CHAPTER 3

CRITICAL THINKING ACTIVITY 3.1

Regarding Example 1, it certainly seems as though further information gathering is required before any action is taken. The 5WH method – who, what, why, where, when and how – applies here. Where has the information come from? How reliable is the source? What are the personal details of Jade? What is known about Jade – any previous police contact? Who owns the property? What type of property is it? There are many intelligence questions to be answered before a course of action is decided upon.

Example 2 in terms of intelligence-led policing is a really good example of a typical reactive investigation. The night shift have arrested two people for burglary, and presented quite a thorough evidence package for the day shift, and there is little for an investigator to do in these circumstances except process them by way of interview and charge if no indication of other offences presents itself.

REFLECTIVE PRACTICE 3.1

If you have compared your answer to the information in the NIM section you should see that Mabel is a vulnerable witness to events. If action was taken which led to officers taking up the ferret pen floor, it would be fairly obvious who had told the police and there could be violent consequences for Mabel. Your intelligence submission should not have contained any personal details of Mabel or any mention of a member of the public and their location. Another approach in this instance would have been to use the information to create an intervention point. It would be prudent in this case to treat the information as 'Official-Sensitive' and use it as a platform to obtain police authorities to generate police intelligence from either a static observation point on the street, using drone technology to observe the house, or any other electronic method. Mabel would then not be involved and neither would her information be needed to make the eventual arrest. The evidence would all be police generated (in line with the legislative parameters of Chapter 2).

CRITICAL THINKING ACTIVITY 3.2

This is a good example of the considerations applied to information when submitted via the NIM and included in the T&C meetings. The information in this example is received quite regularly by all police forces. The information has been inputted into the intelligence system so, aside from the investigatory specifics of who lives where, personal details and various checks which can be made at a routine policing level, broader considerations can be considered within the NIM at the meeting such as:

- is the intelligence reliable and is there any additional information already in the system from previous criminality or association with other criminals?

- what are the resourcing implications of this case if it is to be thoroughly investigated?

- which legislation is to be applied for the offending and for the gathering of any further information thought to be necessary before a search warrant can be applied for?

- are there any health and safety considerations (multiple addresses and information that John Jones may have a firearm)?

- are there any jurisdictional issues to be addressed? (Is this an importation situation due to the amounts of drugs alleged and the fact that ports are being used to smuggle them into the UK?)

REFLECTIVE PRACTICE 3.2

- A white male is suspected to be dealing drugs from a vacant property at 123 ABC Street. He is believed to be called Colin and owns a red Datsun motor car, registered number COL 1N. He is possibly buying drugs in Manchester on Friday (enter date) and usually uses the Datsun for collection trips.

    Notice that there is no mention of the CHIS or the Thursday night party in the intelligence submission. The source of the information should always be protected.

- Checking the information.

i. Local intelligence checks regarding any known Colin who may already be known in the area.

ii. PNC check on the red Datsun motor car COL 1N to find the registered keeper and an address (if it is registered)

iii. Check the address 123 ABC Street for any links.

iv. Possibly check with the CHIS via the relevant department to see if there are any more details which could be useful.

CRITICAL THINKING ACTIVITY 3.3

This information should probably be submitted with at least an Official-Confidential heading if not Secret as it has implications not only for the alleged criminality but potentially for national security as it involves Afghanistan and Iraq.

There are several points within the letter which may offer potential for corroboration as follows.

- Do Jean Kevlar and the company Defence Industries Limited exist?

- Is there any evidence of trading with the countries mentioned?

- Does Fighting Accessories Limited exist?

- Is Fighting Accessories Limited a subsidiary company of Protective Vests for Theatres of War (UK) Limited?

- Has there been any activity in Fighting Accessories Limited at board level to appoint new directors?

- Can the accounts for Fighting Accessories Limited be identified and the bank checked to establish the funds for the company and whether any offshore transfers have occurred?

Although at first sight the information in the letter seems complex, no matter how long or complicated the narrative, apply a systematic approach to the information to draw out facts or suggested truths which can be corroborated or verified. In this example, the four or five different police checks suggested here would quickly demonstrate that the companies and Jean Kevlar are real. The GADPO stages can then be applied to the information at the next T&C meeting if it is decided to take the information forward and to begin an investigation.

CRITICAL THINKING ACTIVITY 3.4

It is important that information which is entered into the intelligence system is sanitised when it needs to be. It should not be possible when reading an intelligence report to identify the source of the information, particularly if it is a person. Although unlikely, there is no guarantee under the Criminal Procedure and Investigations Act 1996 (disclosure) that such information will remain undisclosed to the defendant if court proceedings are undertaken. There is a duty of care to any member of the public, witness or victim to protect their identities. The golden rule is that anyone entering information into the NIM should consider the implications of what is being submitted and to what effect it should be sanitised depending on its type and source. This is vital if a CHIS is involved or, in the circumstances of this example, where a member of the public will provide information but does not want to be exposed as having done so (usually through fear of reprisal).

CRITICAL THINKING ACTIVITY 3.5

Example 1: The security classification here is straightforward. It is Official. Details of the off-duty police officer would not be included in the body of the information. The information itself is simply reporting a sighting and a location of a vehicle belonging to a known criminal.

Example 2: This information is far more complex and there is a potential risk to the source of the information. Within the information are several factors which could affect how it is graded, such as the Hells Angels connection (organised crime), a possible terrorist angle with the high-powered rifle (potential risk to national security), the risk to the woman providing the information (risk to life) and whether it could be tracked back to her if any arrests were ever made. It seems to require more protection than 'Official' and possibly merits a 'Secret' classification for its initial submission to restrict it to particular personnel for the reasons explained here.

CHECK YOUR KNOWLEDGE

1. Intelligence-led policing is a term originally applied to mean an approach to reducing crime which moved away from reactive (retrospective) investigations to ones based upon analysed information (intelligence).

2. Strategic assessment is used to draw inferences of current or longer-term issues and make recommendations. Tactical assessment identifies issues for consideration by a tasking and coordination group which at divisional level usually meets daily to identify immediate problems, review intelligence requirements and consider any emerging trends.

3. The Government Protective Marking Classification system is designed to protect information in accordance with the law.

4. The provenance, assessment and sanitisation of information is important in order to avoid mistakes and erroneous conclusions that could lead to actions such as executing a search warrant at the wrong address.

5. A indicates information which is known directly by the source. B is for information which is offered by a source but not something which the source has directly observed or experienced.

CHAPTER 4

CRITICAL THINKING ACTIVITY 4.1

1. You need to establish what a ROCU is (the regional organised crime unit in your area). You can either ask a colleague, search your force computer system or simply ask your supervisor.

2. Establish a point of contact with the ROCU – is this something your supervisor would know?

3. Establish what is required by the ROCU after speaking to the contact you have identified. Is a report required or simply an electronic transfer of the information you have collated as part of your investigation? This in turn may provide insight as to whether you have any other information to offer their investigation other than your paperwork.

4. Will the ROCU despatch someone to speak to you (effectively a debrief of everything you know) or will it be content with the papers/information you provide?

5. Will your own investigation be concluded by the action the ROCU may or may not take?

Two important points are raised in this activity. First, never assume that someone automatically knows how to do something. Second, when dealing with intelligence or information exchange, define the parameters of what exactly is expected of you.

CRITICAL THINKING ACTIVITY 4.2

There is no right or wrong here. There is only a difference in tactics to be used.

Option 1: Allow the cash delivery vehicle to drive a short distance away from your area before having a marked patrol car intercept it and discover the cash money, perhaps arresting the driver for money laundering.

Option 2: Follow the known drug vehicle containing the cash money to the motorway services and watch the exchange. Then follow the car collecting the money to attempt to find the origin of the drug supply after allowing the exchange to take place.

Option 3: At the point of the money exchanging from the delivery vehicle to the collection vehicle, detain and arrest drivers/passengers of both cars (risking that the drugs are actually inside the second vehicle.

You can see there are several options presenting themselves and this list is not exhaustive. What is does demonstrate is a difference in tactical options which can be considered on information which, on the face of it, seems fairly straightforward.

CRITICAL THINKING ACTIVITY 4.3

Policing checks would be the first and obvious grouping to use to establish exactly who the person is, whether he has any previous convictions or if any information is already held on him. PNC checks may also reveal any motor vehicles registered to him. Address inquiries may provide further context to who the person is and a snapshot of the life being led. All of these details are information. However, the police checks conducted so far do not mean the current information received is accurate. The logical thing to do would be to deploy under the surveillance grouping, and establish an observation point in the vicinity of the nightclub to observe his behaviour and to witness him dealing drugs (see Chapter 2). Police checks can only go so far and other tools such as surveillance may need to be used to convert information or intelligence into evidence.

REFLECTIVE PRACTICE 4.2

The information from the former CHIS seemed to be a repetition of that provided for the actual case in the first place and no credence was put to it to begin with. Officers then persuaded supervisors to check the rental van once more just to be certain as the CHIS was so adamant that 10 kilos had been missed on the original search. The rental company was contacted, and the van surrendered to police. This time the van was manually deconstructed, and no dog used. After some hours a further 10 kilos were found in the roof of the van in a specially constructed hidey hole. Imagine if you had hired the van, were stopped by police and 10 kilos of cannabis resin was found in the roof space. Do you think anyone would believe you were not responsible? This was a lucky escape for over 40 people who had hired the van, including for trips abroad, since it was first searched by police. The lesson here is that even when information seems to have been exhausted (closing the first investigation successfully), rumour and seeming implausibility still need checking thoroughly. All information needs to be considered objectively.

CRITICAL THINKING ACTIVITY 4.4

You always have two immediate choices where foreign inquiries are made.

- You can contact the law enforcement agency concerned using an NCA international liaison officer, a scheme which covers more than 130 countries (National Crime Agency, 2022b). Any information received via this system is a courtesy and not evidence. An ILOR would be required if an evidential path is chosen and a formal application for the evidence would have to be made. The advantage is that you would know the evidence or the information exists as the police have already confirmed it via the NCA.

- You could formally apply on finding the information for an ILOR to convert it to evidence (see Chapter 6). You would not be certain of whether any other information exists or not. You also need to be aware that any inquiry not listed on a properly authorised ILOR will not be granted. If you find something else out after your initial ILOR has been approved and actioned, you will usually have to submit a second ILOR. The golden rule is to wait until you think you have all the relevant inquiries together before submitting to the CPS.

There is a third choice in this example and that is to approach the British Embassy to see if they have any information about your suspect. In some countries, and Thailand is one of them, there is sometimes a His Majesty's Revenue and Customs officer stationed there and the embassy in some cases retains its own intelligence on British nationals in certain, if not all, countries. You may be able to access this information via the British Embassy. It still does not alter the basic rule of thumb that for any official usable information from a foreign jurisdiction, an ILOR will be required (including for the Channel Islands and the Isle of Man).

Regarding the cryptocurrency used in the transaction, your force cybercrime unit may be able to retrieve evidence of the transaction(s), if not the identity of the person(s) who made it. It is likely that an ILOR would not be required for this action in the first instance. The second an overseas jurisdiction becomes involved, and where information is formally required, the situation reverts back to an ILOR course of action.

CHECK YOUR KNOWLEDGE

1. There are **six** tiers of policing

2.

    i. Standard initial police checks.

    ii. Victims and witnesses.

    iii. Communications.

    iv. Vehicles.

    v. Travel.

3. Without context you do not know if the information you have is pertinent or valuable.

4. The International Crime Coordination Centre is a centre for UK policing to tackle transnational crime and provides a knowledge hub for operational police officers.

5. An international letter of request is required where evidence is needed from abroad, usually processed by the prosecutor on behalf of the investigator(s).

CHAPTER 5

EVIDENCE-BASED POLICING

The fact that the information was old should not prevent it from being checked. The detectives who dismissed the information as gossip or the ramblings of a drunken man were showing bias in all of its forms. They approached the information with their pre-conceived idea that it was drunken rumour and then ignored it. The detective who pursued the information was right to do so and you can see the result.

The information was put through an analytical process whereby enough of it could be underpinned by fact (the old property and the imminent release of Simon) and this led to a case for the static observations to be granted. Investigators should not ignore information despite the circumstances in which it originates.

CRITICAL THINKING ACTIVITY 5.1

Whether you realise it or not, you are using a rudimentary intelligence cycle for your decision making. You collate information in this situation as it happens and make real-time decisions based upon the intelligence conclusions you reach.

- You observe the two men.

- They run off (**new information**) and you chase (**outcome**), observing the dropped items and the smashed window (**new information and further consideration**).

- You see one man entering a block of flats (**new information**).

- You gain entry to the reception/foyer area. You decide to enter (**outcome**).

- A resident provides additional information (**new information and further consideration**).

- You consider the information (**analysis of information** so far).

- You liaise with your colleague regarding your powers (**consider what else is relevant or required**).

- The resident has described a man similar to the one you saw, out of breath and wearing the same clothing, entering Flat 4 (**cross-checking and confirming all intelligence known** so far).

After consideration of information and powers you decide you have a power of entry to the flat and when the woman answers the door you politely move her aside, enter the flat and find the man you chased hiding in a cupboard (**intervention point**). You arrest the man on suspicion of committing burglary and theft (**outcome**).

POLICING SPOTLIGHT: OLD INFORMATION AND A NEW PAIR OF EYES

The underlying point being made in this real example is to thoroughly check the information you have collected or provided. If someone else is providing the information you will have an idea of how it was obtained or what use it can be put to. You may, as in this example, already possess a means to arrest and prosecute the criminal. Recognising the material and evaluating it properly is the difficult bit.

REFLECTIVE PRACTICE 5.1

Hopefully, you have reflected that this is a badly written piece of information which the officer has submitted as an intelligence item. The witness has been named in the information and there is no attempt to sanitise its origin. The officer finishes with personal comments concerning Sheila's boss and this is irrelevant in every respect.

The intelligence item should read something like this.

Regarding the fight at Flamingo Park nightclub, 0140hrs Wednesday 12 February 2022, information has been received to the effect that the man responsible for the assault is called Albert Smythe. He is believed to work for a company called Smythe Logistics, which is based at 123 ABC Street, ABC town.

You can see the difference in what is written. In this example, Sheila cannot be identified. There were hundreds of people at the event and the information could have come from any one of them. This way there is no risk of Sheila's personal details falling into the hands of the suspect or defendant as the information has been properly sanitised.

REFLECTIVE PRACTICE 5.2

If you responded in real life as you responded to the man for the purposes of this exercise, you would have made a wrongful arrest.

As the officer in this example, you were led by confirmation bias throughout the incident.

- You convince yourself that the description fits the one circulated over the radio despite different coloured trousers.

- The man is out of breath and therefore must be lying (as you have already made your mind up that the man fits the description). The fact he stated he was running for the bus appears to be ignored.

- You take note of the ACAB tattoo and this is the final piece which suggests in an already made-up mind that the man is anti-police, will not be telling the truth and is probably the man from the incident, all things considered.

- The final piece is the PNC check which provides information that the man has previous convictions for assault.

CRITICAL THINKING ACTIVITY 5.2

Yes, the SARA model could be deployed in these circumstances. In practice it is likely that any affected parties or community groups could be invited to a meeting to consider possibilities regarding lines of available action and what the general community consensus is (scanning). Once these had been identified it could be determined whether any additional information/research is required, what that might look like and a working hypothesis developed (analysis). Investigation could be made if required into any similar instances in your force area or in neighbouring forces and what is being or was done about such situations. Then a plan could be developed based on the evidence available (the response). Finally, if action was eventually taken, was the action successful and how can its effectiveness be ensured going forwards?

CHECK YOUR KNOWLEDGE

1. Any three from this list:

   i. Identify the problem you are trying to solve or the objective you are attempting to attain.

   ii. Do not assume anything. Let the information speak for itself.

   iii. Do not approach any information with a pre-conceived notion of what it will tell you.

   iv. Do not jump to conclusions based on the first piece(s) of information you consider.

   v. Do not pick and choose which pieces of intelligence you see as favourable to your investigation and ignore the rest.

   vi. Do not conceal or avoid information simply because it does not fit your idea of what appears to be happening in an investigation.

   vii. Do not rely on personal or group biases and ignore outside influences such as media.

   vii. Do not make information 'fit' a set of circumstances. It will either confirm or deny your position without your assistance in bending it to your will.

ix. Do not dismiss information because it contradicts your current position.

x. Develop and prepare recommendations from your evaluation of all of the information, no matter whether aligned with or contradictory to the investigation. Present your evaluation in the 'round'.

2. Scanning, Analysis, Response and Assessment.

3. (i) Cognitive bias; (ii) confirmation bias; and (iii) self-serving bias.

4. Information need to be sanitised so as not to expose the source of it and protect individuals who may have provided it.

5.

i. Information gathering.

ii. Analysis.

iii. Outcome.

iv. Dissemination.

v. Decision making and deployment.

CHAPTER 6

CRITICAL THINKING ACTIVITY 6.1

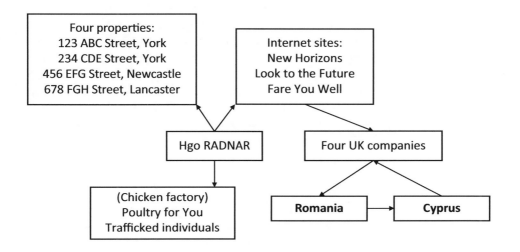

This is a basic chart which illustrates the salient points of the information you want to discuss at your briefing. Using the I2 program or similar software, it is possible to create an in-depth picture of the information in any investigation. Even with this basic drawing of the information, it is immediately clear what is happening. Your audience, be it senior officers, fellow investigators or even a courtroom jury, simply has to follow the arrows to follow your information.

REFLECTIVE PRACTICE 6.1

SCENARIO 1

This is a straightforward breach of the rules and regulations concerning data handling. On no account should police information be used for personal reasons. Access to such information as a police officer is relatively simple and all officers can access the Police National Computer. Never check anyone as a favour or for your own benefit. It is illegal and you will lose your job.

SCENARIO 2

This scenario may seem innocuous, but PC Smith uses the force communications system (via his radio) to alert his partner regarding an ongoing policing situation and real-time information. There is no guarantee that such information will not be relayed to anyone else and suddenly alert the media to an 'inside scoop'. This may seem unlikely, but it has happened in the past.

CRITICAL THINKING ACTIVITY 6.2

All of the agencies involved arranged a meeting to first of all establish exactly how they could assist the investigation. Once this was understood by all the parties present (12 different agencies involved), an MOU was drawn up which specified exactly what each agency would do and how. An ISA was also produced, which allowed personal information to be passed on an intelligence basis from one agency to another but all of which could be passed to the police investigation team. For example, the Department for Work and Pensions attended and were crucial to the investigation. Personal information was required concerning a false benefit account which had been set up by traffickers so that production orders (documents forcing banks to reveal information to the police) could be applied for at the Crown Court.

REFLECTIVE PRACTICE 6.2

The simple answer is that, based upon this scenario, the police force concerned would have to comply with the request. The information is statistical in nature, does not relate to any ongoing investigations and, as long as it does not cost much to furnish the information, there is no real reason not to provide it.

CRITICAL THINKING ACTIVITY 6.3

Request 1 – the information sought is subject to an ongoing court case. It is therefore something which cannot be released under an FOI request and the request can be denied on those grounds.

Request 2 – the request wants a lot of information, some of which may not be already available or in a form which is easily retrievable. This request is likely to be rejected on that basis. However, in the spirit of public co-operation it is likely that any police force receiving such a lengthy request might as a gesture of goodwill supply basic cash detention figures and the values forfeited. This information definitely would be available as these figures are recorded centrally in London on a system called the Joint Asset Recovery Database (JARD).

CHECK YOUR KNOWLEDGE

1. A MOPI system is required to manage police information effectively and transparently in an easily recoverable fashion.

2. [missing]

3. A memorandum of understanding is usually issued when more than one agency is involved and sets out who should do what in order to be clear and not duplicate enquiries.

4. An information sharing agreement ensures that information can be exchanged between agencies and that it will be used for policing purposes.

5.

- **M**edia strategy

- **A**pplication of information gathering methods

- **T**asking and co-ordination

- **R**isk assessment

- **I**nvestigation plan

- **C**lear communication

- **E**valuation

- **S**takeholders

REFERENCES

Archer, B and Ellison, G (2023) *Police Procedure and Evidence in the Criminal Justice System*. St Albans: Critical Publishing.

Arizona State University (2022) The SARA Model. [online] Available at: https://popcenter. asu.edu/content/sara-model-0 (accessed 3 February 2023).

Association of Chief Police Officers (ACPO) (2005) *Guidance on the National Intelligence Model*. Bedford: National Centre for Policing Excellence. [online] Available at: https://whereis mydata.files.wordpress.com/2009/01/national-intelligence-model-20051.pdf (accessed 3 February 2023).

Bichard, M (2004) *The Bichard Inquiry Report*. HC653. London: The Stationery Office.

Blackstone, W (1778) *Commentaries on the Laws of England*. Vol 1. London: Clarendon Press.

Burton, S and McGregor, M (2018) Enhancing SARA: A New Approach in an Increasingly Complex World. *Crime Science*, 7(4). [online] Available at: https://crimesciencejournal. biomedcentral.com/articles/10.1186/s40163-018-0078-4# (accessed 3 February 2023).

Byford, L (1981) *The Yorkshire Ripper Case: Review of the Investigation of the Case by Lawrence Byford, Her Majesty's Inspector of Constabulary*. London: Home Office. [online] Available at: www.gov.uk/government/publications/sir-lawrence-byford-report-into-the-police-handling-of-the-yorkshire-ripper-case (accessed 3 February 2023).

Cabinet Office (2018) *Government Security Classifications*. Version 1.1. [online] Available at: https://assets.publishing.service.gov.uk/government/uploads/system/uploads/attachme nt_data/file/715778/May-2018_Government-Security-Classifications-2.pdf (accessed 3 February 2023).

Ciampaglia, G and Menczer, F (2018) Biases Make People Vulnerable to Misinformation Spread by Social Media. *The Conversation*, June 2018. [online] Available at: https://thec onversation.com/misinformation-and-biases-infect-social-media-both-intentionally-and-accidentally-97148 (accessed 3 February 2023).

College of Policing (2013) Intelligence Strategy. [online] Available at: www.college. police.uk/app/investigation/investigative-strategies/intelligence-strategy (accessed 3 February 2023).

College of Policing (2020) Authorised Professional Practice: Information Sharing. [online] Available at: www.college.police.uk/app/information-management/information-sharing (accessed 3 February 2023).

College of Policing (2022a) Authorised Professional Practice. [online] Available at: www.college.police.uk/app/intelligence-management/intelligence-report.

College of Policing (2022b) Intelligence Products. [online] Available at: www.college.police. uk/app/intelligence-management/intelligence-products (accessed 3 February 2023).

College of Policing (2022c) Collection and Recording. [online] Available at: www.college. police.uk/app/information-management/management-police-information/collection-and-recording (accessed 3 February 2023).

College of Policing (2022d) *Disrupting Serious and Organised Criminals: Menu of Tactics*. [online] Available at: https://assets.college.police.uk/s3fs-public/2022-03/Menu_of_ tactics.pdf (accessed 3 February 2023).

College of Policing (2022e) International Investigation Useful Contacts. [online] Available at: www.college.police.uk/app/investigation/international/international-investigation-useful-contacts (accessed 3 February 2023).

College of Policing (2022f) Problem-oriented Policing. [online] Available at: www. college.police.uk/research/crime-reduction-toolkit/problem-oriented-policing (accessed 3 February 2023).

College of Policing (2023) Innovation. [online] Available at: www.college.police.uk/support-forces/innovation (accessed 7 March 2023).

Coyne, J W and Bell, P (2011) The Role of Strategic Intelligence in Anticipating Transnational Organised Crime: A Literary Review. *International Journal of Law, Crime and Justice*, 39(1): 60–78.

Crown Prosecution Service (2017) Dealing with Surveillance Authorisations. [online] Available at: www.cps.gov.uk/legal-guidance/disclosure-manual-chapter-26-dealing-surve illance-authorisations (accessed 3 February 2023).

Crown Prosecution Service (2021) Disclosure Manual: Chapter 31 – Cases using Holmes. [online] Available at: www.cps.gov.uk/legal-guidance/disclosure-manual-chapter-31-cases-using-holmes (accessed 18 October 2022).

Eurojust (2022) Joint Investigation Teams. [online] Available at: www.eurojust.europa.eu/ judicial-cooperation/instruments/joint-investigation-teams (accessed 3 February 2023).

Federal Bureau of Investigation (FBI) (2022) Intelligence Branch of the FBI. [online] Available at: https://psu.pb.unizin.org/hls476/chapter/chapter-1 (accessed 3 February 2023).

Flood, B and Gaspar, R (2009) Strategic Aspects of the UK National Intelligence Model. In Ratcliffe, J (ed) *Strategic Thinking in Criminal Intelligence* (pp 46–65). 2nd ed. New South Wales: Federation Press.

GCHQ (2022) Mission. [online] Available at: www.gchq.gov.uk/section/mission/overview (accessed 3 February 2023).

Guidetti, R (2009) Collaborative Intelligence Production. In Ratcliffe, J (ed) *Strategic Thinking in Criminal Intelligence* (pp 222–47). 2nd ed. New South Wales: Federation Press.

Heldon, C E (2009) Exploratory Analysis Tools. In Ratcliffe, J H (ed) *Strategic Thinking in Criminal Intelligence* (pp 124–56). 2nd ed. New South Wales: The Federation Press.

HM Government (2018) *CONTEST: The United Kingdom's Strategy for Countering Terrorism.* [online] Available at: https://assets.publishing.service.gov.uk/government/uploads/system/uploads/attachment_data/file/714404/060618_CCS207_CCS0218929798-1_CONTEST_3.0_PRINT.PDF (accessed 3 February 2023).

House of Lords (2008) *European Union – Twenty-Ninth Report.* London: UK Parliament. [online] Available at: https://publications.parliament.uk/pa/ld200708/ldselect/ldeucom/183/18302.htm (accessed 3 February 2023).

Hughes, C (2021) *Financial Investigation: Establishing the Principles of a Generic and Effective Philosophy.* Unpublished doctoral thesis. Derby: University of Derby.

Investigatory Powers Commissioner's Office (IPCO) (2022) Investigatory Powers. [online] Available at: www.ipco.org.uk/investigatory-powers (accessed 3 February 2023).

Ling, R (2020) Confirmation Bias in the Era of Mobile News Consumption: The Social and Psychological Dimensions. *Digital Journalism,* 8(5): 596–604.

Lyons, B J (2015) Feds Pay $134,000 to Settle DEA Agent's Fake Facebook Case. [online] Available at: www.timesunion.com/news/article/Feds-pay-134k-to-woman-whose-ID-used-by-DEA-on-6027904.php (accessed 3 February 2023).

Mason, G (2020) The Yorkshire Ripper: The Case That Led to the HOLMES System. *Police Oracle,* November 2020. [online] Available at: www.policeoracle.com/news/investigation/2020/Nov/13/the-yorkshire-ripper--the-case-that-led-to-the-holmes-system-_106190.html/news (accessed 3 February 2023).

Merriam-Webster (2022) 'Information'. [online] Available at: www.merriam-webster.com/dictionary/information (accessed 3 February 2023).

National Centre for Policing Excellence (2005a) *Guidance on the National Intelligence Model*. [online] Available at: https://whereismydata.files.wordpress.com/2009/01/national-intelligence-model-20051.pdf (accessed 3 February 2023).

National Centre for Policing Excellence (2005b) *Code of Practice on the Management of Police Information*. [online] Available at: https://library.college.police.uk/docs/APPref/Management-of-Police-Information.pdf (accessed 3 February 2023).

National Crime Agency (2015) *The NCA Commitment to Working in Partnership with Police and Crime Commissioners*. [online] Available at: www.nationalcrimeagency.gov.uk/who-we-are/publications/34-the-nca-commitment-to-working-in-partnership-with-pccs/file (accessed 3 February 2023).

National Crime Agency (2022a) Intelligence: Enhancing the Picture of Serious and Organised Crime Affecting the UK. [online] Available at: www.nationalcrimeagency.gov.uk/what-we-do/how-we-work/intelligence-enhancing-the-picture-of-serious-organised-crime-affecting-the-uk (accessed 3 February 2023).

National Crime Agency (2022b) International Network. [online] Available at: www.nationalcrimeagency.gov.uk/what-we-do/how-we-work/providing-specialist-capabilities-for-law-enforcement/international-network (accessed 3 February 2023).

Office for National Statistics (ONS) (2022) Crime and Justice. [online] Available at: www.ons.gov.uk/peoplepopulationandcommunity/crimeandjustice (accessed 3 February 2023).

Petersen, M (2005) *Intelligence-led Policing: The New Intelligence Architecture*. Washington: United States Department of Justice. [online] Available at: www.ojp.gov/pdffiles1/bja/210681.pdf (accessed 3 February 2023).

Ratcliffe, J H (ed) (2009) *Strategic Thinking in Criminal Intelligence*. New South Wales: The Federation Press.

Ribaux, O, Girod, A, Walsh, S J, Margot, P, Mizrahi, S and Clivaz, V (2003) Forensic Intelligence and Crime Analysis. *Law, Probability and Risk*, 2(1): 47–60.

Richards, J (2010) *The Art and Science of Intelligence*. Oxford: Oxford University Press.

Simple Psychology (2022) What Is Cognitive Bias? [online] Available at: www.simply psychology.org/cognitive-bias.html (accessed 3 February 2023).

Spooner, E, Hughes, C and Jones, P (2022) *Police Research and Evidence-Based Policing*. St Albans: Critical Publishing.

United Nations Office on Drugs and Crime (UNODC) (2011) *Criminal Intelligence Manual for Analysts*. [online] Available at: www.unodc.org/documents/organized-crime/Law-Enforcem ent/Criminal_Intelligence_for_Analysts.pdf (accessed 3 February 2023).

Warner, M (2002) Wanted: A Definition of 'Intelligence'. *Studies in Intelligence*, 46(3). Washington, DC: CIA. [online] Available at: www.cia.gov/resources/csi/studies-in-intelligence/archives/vol-46-no-3/wanted-a-definition-of-intelligence (accessed 7 March 2023).

INDEX

Note: Page numbers in **bold** denote tables.